T0405891

The Dizziness of Freedom in Kierkegaard and Sartre

Riccardo Pugliese

The Dizziness of Freedom in Kierkegaard and Sartre

palgrave
macmillan

Riccardo Pugliese
Rome, Italy

ISBN 978-3-031-38137-9   ISBN 978-3-031-38138-6   (eBook)
https://doi.org/10.1007/978-3-031-38138-6

This Palgrave Macmillan imprint is published by the registered company Springer Nature Switzerland AG.
The registered company address is: Gewerbestrasse 11, 6330 Cham, Switzerland

Preface: The Sense of Possibility

In the history of Western culture, possibility seems a lateral and secondary space, a dense and intricate forest, at the edge of the straight roads of necessity and the vast grassy expanses of reality. Possibility drags one along a path that unfolds over fluid, changing, and tumultuous vistas, boundless horizons in which things suddenly no longer appear for what they are and we ourselves are surprised to become different, slipping from other to other, caught in the vortex of a bewildering vertigo. Yet, if reality is confirmed as the dimension connoted by an evidence of truth that imposes itself in opposition to what is false or, if you will, as the blunt consistency of objectivity that stands in the way of what is purely subjective and, finally, as the affirmative fullness of the positive that excludes the negative, possibility manifests itself, on the other hand, as the mode, proper and all-encompassing, of meaning.

Science and philosophical thought in general regard possibility as a mere *shadow* of reality, that is, as a *non-reality* that the affirmation of the *fact of the real* continually dissolves. Yet, to only a more careful and philosophically equipped gaze, it becomes clear that possibility, even on a strictly logical level, contains both the real (what Leibniz called the realm of *truths of fact*) and the necessary (the Leibnizian *truths of reason*). The possible does not exclude the possibilities it contemplates. The logical formula of possibility, which is also the strategic formula of dialectics in the tradition of thought from Heraclitus to Hegel, affirms both x and *non-x*. Here negation should not be conceived as that which excludes x from its other (*non-x*), but as the dividing line of two fields that it simultaneously helps to generate and hold together in a new and broader perspective of inclusion. The possible is to be understood as a capacity, as a potential for self-assertion and co-assertion, as a vital dynamism that runs through all things and binds them together in the hospitable frame of meaning.

The scientific and philosophical confinement of possibility outside of reality and, consequently, the absolutization of the latter, this is the formal characteristic of all ideological reductionism, conceal the indisputable experiential and historical fact that, as symbolic animals and by virtue of the theatricality of our consciousness, *we are at once in reality and in possibility.*

After all, it is an indisputable clinical fact that, when insanity manifests itself in its most dramatic form, the subject completely loses that capacity to *simulate* that allows access to the world of possibility. Rather, the madman, crushed in the dimension of reality *alone*, experiences, in the suffering flesh of his barren life, the impossible, that is, a world composed only of necessity. In short, the madmen, to put it jokingly, take themselves extremely seriously. Madness and the existential condition of the insane manifest, in the most painful way, the essence of the contradiction inherent in isolation, univocity, and the consequent absolutization of the field of reality and its reduction to a single level. In psychosis, both in manic-depressive and in schizophrenic psychosis, the ability to understand certain situations "as if" is severely impaired or compromised. It follows that playful and dramaturgical practices, which induce patients to simulate, appear today to be an effective therapeutic tool to take the insane out of the exclusive cage not only of *their* reality, but of *one* reality. That is to say, of that *idiotism of reality* that is the first anomaly to be healed in those insane people who simply *want more* of what even so-called normal people want. It is a matter, in the words of Robert Musil's *The Man Without Qualities*, of discerning, alongside and indeed inscribed at the heart of the sense of reality, *the sense of possibility*, "which could also be defined as the ability to think everything that could equally be."[1]

While Descartes had placed the subject's actions under the adaptive banner of that third maxim of "provisional morality," which reads "change your desires rather than change the order of the world,"[2] modern fictional characters, who traverse the history of European theater and novel with

---

[1] R. Musil, *Der Mann ohne Eigenschaften* (1930–1933; 1942), it. tr., *L'uomo senza qualità*, in 2 voll., Einaudi, Torino 1957, vol. 1, p. 12.

[2] R. Descartes, *Discours de la méthode* (1637), III; it. tr., *Discorso sul metodo*, in Id., Opere, in 4 voll., Laterza, Roma-Bari 2000, vol. 1, p. 307.

cheerful and euphoric boldness, are perfect spoilers of the un-transform-ability of the real and of those in universities, academies, and parliaments who champion it. These gentlemen are convinced, as Kundera noted, "that truth is self-evident, that all men must think the same thing and that they themselves are exactly what they think they are. But man becomes an individual precisely when he loses the certainty of truth and the unanimous consent of others."[3] The theatricality of consciousness opens up reality to the dialectic of the possible and teaches that passion of possibility of which Kierkegaard spoke when recounting his experiences as a spectator at the Königstädter Theater in Berlin, where, projecting himself on the stage, "the individual has a quantity of shadows that all resemble him and are equally entitled to coincide momentarily with himself."[4]

The main mode in which the eminent character of culture is expressed is neither the real nor the necessary, but rather, taking up Northrop Frye's suggestion, the virtuality of the *possible*. Compared to *totalitarian syntheses* of reality, culture, which "can be provisionally defined as an organic complex of imaginative hypotheses within a society and its traditions," sediments above all that which power (and the knowledge reflected in it) excludes, preparing "in some way its revenge."[5] Thus, possibility is, from the earliest evidence of culture, the self-therapeutic device by which humans have preserved the richness of their singular and collective experience from the adaptive flattening of instrumental rationality on the fatality of the world. Indeed, we might say that human beings *have a world* and are not *simply in the world* precisely because they are able to produce this non-adaptive differential. What prevents the human mind from turning into a mere calculating, artificially reproducible mechanism—the infamous "artificial intelligence" of contemporary science fiction mythology and today's news reporting in the service of astute Nasdaq speculators—lies precisely in the faculty of generating ineradicable paradoxes. As William Fry has written, "[T]he presence of paradox seems to confer more richness on life. Paradox is found in play, ritual, dreams, folklore, creations of the imagination, art, theater, psychotherapy and humor. Indeed, most of what gives comfort and pleasure to human life

---

[3] M. Kundera, *L'art du roman. Essai* (1986); it. tr., *L'arte del romanzo. Saggio*, Adelphi, Milano 1988, p. 220.

[4] S. Kierkegaard, *Gjentagelsen* (1843); it. tr., *La ripetizione*, Rizzoli, Milano 2000, p. 43.

[5] N. Frye, *Anatomy of Criticism. Four Essays* (1957); it. tr., *Anatomia della critica. Quattro saggi*, Einaudi, Torino 2000, p. 166.

falls into these categories, and paradox seems to be essential to each of these phenomena."[6]

The essence of paradox is the undecidable coexistence of two contradictory perspectives that, therefore, cannot be together. But this incompatibility manifests itself in reality alone, where the logical-calculative systems enter a vicious circle and get stuck or simply move on without realizing it, certainly not in possibility. Reality, in fact, is shaped according to the *either/or* rule: true or false; real or unreal; sane or insane. However, if this alone were reality, the paradox would not even arise, as in the algorithms of so-called intelligent systems. The impossibility of contradiction would result in the impossibility of contradicting oneself. Instead, there is already in reality, that is, in the way the structure of our being conceives it, an opening from which stems the reversal of the exclusive rule of the either/or, to the inclusive rule of *both/and* (true and false; real and unreal; sane and insane). This is what psychoanalysis has indicated as the logic governing the dimension of the unconscious, but which appears in direct relation to that constitutive metaphoricity of the human being that is rooted in the dramaturgical structure of consciousness. In consciousness we simulate, but this simulation is not to be understood as a determined gesture or as an artifice, but as that mode in which a double movement is accomplished: on the one hand, reality is made possible, renouncing its unquestionability, while on the other hand, possibility is realized, making it compatible with reality. What gives pleasure and comfort to human life—in a word, that which gives it *meaning*—and which, in the course of humanity's cultural adventure, has produced the grand symbolic performances of religion and art, but also the original cognitive challenge from which the enterprise of science moves, can be traced back to this double movement that transforms the *either/or* of instrumental rationality and its operative performances into the *both/and* of metaphorical and imaginative reason.

However, the effects of possibility on reality do not stop at this opening. The most arduous passage that possibility suggests is the one that from the contradictory coexistence of the two positive and identifiable dimensions— the *both/and*, mentioned above, arrives at the *neither/nor*, that is, at the compossible coexistence of two negatives (neither true nor false, neither real nor unreal, neither sane nor insane), where the sense of things seems

---

[6]W. F. Fry, *Sweet Madness* (1963); it. tr., *Una dolce follia. L'umorismo e i suoi paradossi*, Raffaello Cortina Editore, Milano 2001, p. 185.

lost. After all, when Freud, in *Jokes and Their Relation to the Unconscious*, tells the famous little story of the leaky cauldron, he is confronting us with the same structure.[7] A man lends a cauldron and when it is returned to him he complains that it has a hole in it. Then, the guy who borrowed it defends himself by replying that it is not true, rather that the cauldron was already leaking and that, moreover, he did not borrow any cauldron. It is evident that his answer implies the paradox of contradiction if we are to choose one of the three versions, which he gives in succession, and which are mutually exclusive (*either/or*). However, while the first two are compossible (*both/and*) and therefore realizable, the third has the characteristic of calling into question the tale itself and, therefore, the very background of reality on which the tale rests, for if no cauldron was ever lent, it cannot have been either intact nor leaking (neither/nor). But, if even the impossible is possible, then one has reached the logical apex of the absurd, but at the same time one savors in a moment the liberation from all constraints.

It is precisely this situation, in landing at the coexistence of two negatives, that opens up the possibility of an ethics of freedom.[8] It is in the negation that the human being is affirmed as such, when he affirms himself as that which can distance itself from what is given, can transcend itself, can develop itself, and thus can become man. Without this step of negation, we remain entangled in reality as the only dimension of truth, objectivity, and positivity.

To conclude, only a reality mottled with possibilities can be called a world, or rather worlds, because there are as many of them as there are singularities that experience their countless variations. Sometimes these are very different worlds with few common tangents, sometimes almost overlapping, but still different in what remains essential. We can subject a human being to the most heinous violence and cruelty, but the greatest violence will always be that which in life takes away the world, that is, possibility, which pins man on reality alone, which reduces him or her to living from day to day, hour to hour, not knowing whether there will be tomorrow or knowing that tomorrow will be exactly the same as today.

---

[7] See P. A. Rovatti, *Il paiolo bucato. La nostra condizione paradossale*, Raffaello Cortina Editore, Milano 1998.

[8] I. Valent, *L'etica della possibilità* (2002), in Id., *Panta diapànton. Scritti teorici su follia e cura*, a c. di G. Valent, in *Opere di Italo Valent* (in 6 voll.), a c. di A. Tagliapietra, vol. VI, Moretti & Vitali, Bergamo 2009, pp. 319–335.

Reducing a person to a thing means denying him the world. Animals and plants also have a world, but for the most part this is foreign to us, and we come to recognize and share it only with those who look like us, so we generally believe that they have no world. But only things have no world. This is what happened in the terrible concentration camp experiences of the twentieth century, in the *Lager*, in the *Gulag*. This is what happens, everywhere and at all times, when the singularity of a human being is completely erased and in its place remains only the bureaucratic recurrence of a series, the anonymous identity of a general classification, the treatment of women and men as if they were mere statistics, that is, numbers with no more world.

Rome, Italy   Andrea Tagliapietra

CONTENTS

CHAPTER 1

Existence as Possibility

Abstract This chapter serves as a general introduction on the themes of freedom, choice, and responsibility in their philosophical formulation. Special emphasis will be given to the concept of existence as possibility in Kierkegaard and its development throughout one of his seminal works, *Either/Or* (1843).

Keywords Kierkegaard • Existence • Choice • Possibility • *Either/Or* • Personality

What does it mean to be free? Is there a definitive philosophical determination for this concept? This book attempts to shed light on the topic of freedom as the ontological foundation of modern man through its formulation since Hegel. The first part of the book will investigate the relationship between freedom and possibility in Kierkegaard, while the second dwells on the idea of freedom as condemnation as it was conceived by the philosopher who most radicalized its scope: Jean-Paul Sartre.[1]

No one like Søren Kierkegaard has been able to tether the understanding of the entire human existence to the category of possibility, while at the same time accentuating its negative and paralyzing aspect. The concept of possibility in the work of the Danish philosopher should be analyzed by making explicit its relationship with freedom. The idea of possibility inherent in everyone, may it be real or transcendental, had already been recognized by Immanuel Kant, who had highlighted its positive connotation. Kant saw possibility as a human capacity, which, while limited, finds its validity in the limits themselves. Kierkegaard is the first to analyze the negative aspect of every possibility that constitutes human existence. Every possibility implies the nullity of what is possible, thus ushering in the threat of nothingness.

In *Stages on Life's Way* (1845) Kierkegaard writes: "What I am is nothingness; this provides me and my genius the satisfaction of preserving my existence at the *zero-point*, between hot and cold, between wisdom and foolishness, between something and nothing as a mere *maybe*." We should note the use of the word "satisfaction" as if Kierkegaard were basking in complacency among the billows of indeterminacy and indecision. Better therefore to drown in an open and comfortably indefinable sea than to dock in an unknown harbor. The *zero-point* embodies permanent indecision, the unstable balance between opposing alternatives that present themselves in the face of any given possibility.[2]

> Every man naturally desires to act in this world according to his own strength, but from this follows in turn the desire to shape his forces in a particular direction, which best suits his individuality. But what is it? [...] It is not a simple fork in the road, but an intersection of ways that radiate in all directions. Here is why it is so difficult to take the right one. Such is perhaps the misfortune of my existence, being interested in too many things, without

---

[1] Some of the most recent studies in this regard: J. Webber, *The Existentialism of Jean-Paul Sartre*, Routledge, New York 2009; R.E. Santoni, *Bad Faith, Good Faith and Authenticity in Sartre's Early Philosophy*, Temple University Press, Philadelphia 1985; J. Simont, *La lutte du maître et de l'esclave dans Cahiers pour une morale et Critique de la raison dialectique*, "Etudes Sartriennes", 4, 1990; D. Detmer, *Freedom as a Value. A critique of the Ethical Theory of Jean-Paul Sartre*, Open Court Publishing Company, Illinois 1988.

[2] See F.C. Fischer, *Die Nullpunkt – Existenz, Dargestelt an der Lebensform Soren Kierkegaards*, München: Beck 1933.

ever arriving at any decision: none of my interests is subordinate to another, but they all hold each other's hand.[3]

For Kierkegaard, existence is not a necessary and guaranteed entity, but a set of possibilities that—as such—compels man to make a choice and imply an ineradicable component of risk. To exist means to choose. Indeed, choice is not a simple manifestation of behavior, but constitutes personality itself, which chooses by living or lives by choosing.[4]

> Could one express with greater precision that freedom of choice is just a nominal expression of freedom? And that the very accentuation of freedom of choice constitutes the loss of freedom itself? The content of freedom is so decisive for freedom, that the truth of freedom of choice is precisely to admit that here there must be no choice, although that itself is a choice.[5]

Kierkegaard's work, significantly titled *Either/Or* (1843), sheds light on two problems: the foundational importance of choice in shaping personality, and the unbridgeable gap between the alternatives of existence. "Choice itself is decisive for personality: through choice personality sinks into the thing chosen, and when it does not choose, it withers in consumption."[6] The Kierkegaardian postulate implies that from choice there is no escape. It is a determination against which the individual must inevitably confront. One is who one chooses to be; this assertion looms with tragic weight on Man. There is no crease, no recess, no dark corner of the mind where he can take shelter. We will see how brilliantly Sartre takes up this point later by exasperating it into the conceit of freedom as condemnation. Choice therefore is an ineradicable component of our persona. In other words, the individual is not what he is but what he chooses to be. Consequently, even the renunciation of choice is a choice, albeit a type of choice by which man renounces himself.

---

[3] S. Kierkegaard, *Diario*, Rizzoli, Milano 2019, [46].

[4] W. Lowrie, *"Existence" as Understood by Kierkegaard and/or Sartre*, "The Sewanee Review", vol. 58, no. 3, 1950, pp. 379–401; P.L. Gardiner, *Kierkegaard: A Very Short Introduction*, Oxford University Press, Oxford 2002, p. 113; N. Abbagnano, *Possibilità e libertà*, Taylor, Torino 1956.

[5] S. Kierkegaard, *Diario*, op. cit., [2148].

[6] S. Kierkegaard, *Aut-Aut: Estetica ed etica nella formazione della personalità*, Mondadori, Milano 2015, p. 10.

The question of choice occupies a central place in Kierkegaard's thought and is closely connected with the three stages of existence (aesthetic, ethical, and religious) under the banner by which man can and must choose to live his life. If *Either/Or* serves Kierkegaard to expound in detail on the first two stages and their respective existential implications, it is especially in the essay *Equilibrium Between the Aesthetic and the Ethical in the Composition of Personality* (1843) that the decisive role of choice according to a given perspective of life is cogently highlighted. Choice becomes the supreme guiding criterion, the beacon of light that guides the individual from a pre-moral condition of indifference toward the adoption of a given behavior. The essay consists of the critique made by Judge Wilhelm, who embodies the quintessential ethical man, to his aesthete friend. Fundamental for understanding the theme of personality in its moral cohesion, the work also underpins the theme of choice in an absolute sense.

From the very first pages, choice is identified by Wilhelm with ethics itself. "What then manifests with my either/or is ethics. Therefore, one cannot yet speak of the choice of something, one cannot yet speak of the reality of what has been chosen, but of the reality of choosing itself."[7] The ethical stage is the moment when man, by choosing to choose, that is, by assuming full responsibility for his own freedom, commits himself to a task to which he remains faithful. The ethical man embraces the repetition that the aesthete has shunned with dismay by chasing what's new at every moment. Instead, he grounds his life on continuity and repeatedly chooses himself and his task. Ethics is also defined by the author of *The Equilibrium* as "that by which [man] becomes what he becomes." This best expresses the essence of all modern ethics since Kierkegaard, that of transformation, growth, and development, while also introducing its founding concept: freedom.

In Greek culture, the genesis of the concept of freedom takes place within the horizon of the πόλις, embodied in the participation of the individual in public decisions. However, its first philosophical meaning defines "free" only those who are self-determined. This self-determination or self-causality, which goes back to Plato and Aristotle (αὐτάρκεια), is taken up by the Stoics and Epicureans, who maintain that actions are free only if they have in themselves their own cause. They speak of freedom while establishing the order of the cosmos as necessary, since this does not

---

[7] Ibid., p. 26.

depend on man. In this perspective Epictetus defines as free the things "in our power" while for Origen, freedom consists in being the cause of one's own acts. The ancient Greeks seek to identify freedom essentially as one's ability to be the cause of their own acts, so as to make oneself independent from any kind of external conditioning. Although timely intuited, the concept of freedom was never fully thematized by the Greek world. Not even its two most influential philosophical voices, Plato in the myth of Er (*Republic*, X) and Aristotle in the *Nicomachean Ethics*, succeed in thinking of it unconditionally, as disengaged from any other determination or as an absolute beginning. The concept of freedom as will is later introduced by Blaise Pascal, who in the *Pensées* (1670) ponders what the self is. More precisely, Pascal poses the question of what the irreducible essence of man might be, that is, his most intrinsic characteristic. The question seemed destined to remain unsolved, but it would be Kierkegaard two centuries later to take it up and answer it. For the Danish philosopher, the essence of man is neither soul nor body but freedom; such is the inalienable and visceral determination without which man is reduced to a thing. It will be Sartre—as we will see—who would repropose the theme, identifying the concept of freedom with that of transcendence and "project." Recovering the Kierkegaardian definition of man as a synthesis of finite and infinite contained in *The Sickness unto Death* (1849), Sartre will conceive the individual as a relationship between giveness and transcendence. Sartre defines the latter as the capacity—exclusively human—to overcome the limit of one's own self-determination and enact itself in a plan for the realization of an absolute self. The exercise of freedom understood in Sartre's terms, consists precisely in overcoming one's own limited and immediate natural condition for the realization of one's own ideality.

For Kierkegaard and Sartre, freedom is constitutive of man, the foundational trait of one's self, the indispensable tool for bringing to light the best version of self. In ethics, man "becomes what he becomes," thus abandoning the constricting limits of his own giveness to realize himself in a long-term project of self-perfection with commitment and constant dedication. The ethical individual is one who is true to himself and to the task he sets out, determined to seek the best version of self. In *The Equilibrium*, Wilhelm reproaches his friend the aesthete for being exactly the opposite, for limiting himself to being "immediately what he is." But what is the meaning of this expression? It means that an individual is what he is, his substance, his nature, his essence.

Since man is then the only existing being capable of redefining his essence, of modifying his own nature, the adverb 'immediately' is meant to specify that the aesthetic in man is everything by which he is what he is as product of (nature, history, etc.), in other words all that for which he is what he is found to be, without his having contributed to it in the least, meaning the essence assigned to him.[8]

Therefore, according to the magistrate Wilhelm, aesthetic indicates the *situation* in which man comes to find himself, in the connotation that will be attributed to it by existentialism. The concept of situation is in fact one of the original formulations of existentialism; I am thrown into the world, Martin Heidegger will say, I am thrown into my situation.

I have this body, I have these relatives, these friends, this homeland, this profession, these relationships with others: that is, I have a determined location within the universe, a specific place in the world, in a word: a situation, or rather my situation. [...] My situation is my concreteness, my configuration or, in Gabriel Marcel's words, my *incarnation*: without it I, as a single person, would not be. The ties that bind me to my situation are very tight, and above all they are essential to me: they are not ties of ownership but of essence.[9]

The aesthetic stage is the form of life in which the individual "is immediately what he is," meaning the behavior of he who, by rejecting any constraint or continued commitment, seeks the fleeting moment of his own realization under the banner of novelty and adventure. Carpe diem, or rather *carpe horam*, is the motto of the aesthete, immediacy, and exteriority its characteristics. The former is, as we have seen, the quality of he who is naturally, genuinely what he is. The latter is proper to one who grounds himself and the meaning of his life on external agents (e.g., wealth), or independent from one's own will (such as beauty, health, talent, or intelligence).

Every man, no matter how unintelligent, however low his position in life, has a natural need to form a conception of life, a representation of the meaning of life and its purpose. [...] But he who sees in enjoyment the meaning and purpose of life, always subjects his life to a condition that either

[8] L. Amoroso, *Maschere kierkegaardiane*, Rosenberg and Sellier, Torino 1990, p. 191.
[9] L. Pareyson, *Studi sull'esistenzialismo*, Sansoni, Firenze 1971, p. 16.

lies outside the individual or is in the individual but in such a way as not to be placed by the individual himself.[10]

Estranged from himself and slave to his own incompleteness, the aesthete tends toward an ephemeral happiness, an illusory and momentary state of affairs, a fleeting flash of lightning in the blackest night. He merely collects pieces of the puzzle of an existence he can never complete. The aesthete aims at the fulfillment of his own desire, lives for it, pursues it with all his might, to the point of annulling himself in it. But his bounty is meager spoils, because it is incapable of quenching his thirst. He is attempting to quell his need for the absolute through an infinite set of finite moments. The inexhaustible desire of the aesthete solely rests on an object until it has exhausted his interest before moving on to another. This cycle goes on forever, since no object, however palatable, can accommodate in itself an unlimited desire. The aesthetic conduct turns out to be fragmentary, haphazard, and unsuccessful, because it is dictated by a misunderstood sense of happiness. The category of the aesthete is multiplicity, but it is a defective and inconclusive one, as opposed to the ethical oneness of he who harmoniously combines and values each individual experience in a higher design. In other words, in the ethical life the individual submits to a form or model of universal behavior, which implies the choice of the "normality" in place of the desire for exceptionality. Such desire compelled the aesthete to make his life a work of art from which monotony is banished in favor of unprecedented emotions. Kierkegaard thus takes up the Kantian concept of the universality of reason and of the absoluteness of the moral law by reiterating that morality is "precisely the general" and, as general, is that which applies to all.

---

[10] S. Kierkegaard, *Aut-Aut*, op. cit., p. 30.

CHAPTER 2

The Despairing Aesthete: The Pioneer of Pain

Abstract The chapter further examines the distinction between aesthetic and ethical life in Kierkegaard's *Either/Or*. In the essay *Equilibrium Between the Aesthetic and the Ethical in the Composition of Personality* (1843), Kierkegaard illustrates what he calls the supreme stage of aesthetic life, which he identifies with desperation itself. This phase of existence embodies the disenchantment of aesthetic life and immediately precedes the ethical realm. A conscious effort to choose one's life is the only viable option to transition from the precarious aesthetic stage to the ethical one, predicated upon commitment.

Keywords Kierkegaard • Existence • Desperation • Nothingness • Truth • Choice

The typology of the aesthete Wilhelm addresses in *Either/Or* is profoundly different from that of the ordinary aesthete described above. The figure to whom Kierkegaard (through Wilhelm) is referring to here is the higher and more complex one of the despairing aesthete.

> There still remains, however, a stage, a conception of aesthetic life, the finest and most aristocratic of all; [...] this last conception of life is despair itself. It is a conception of aesthetic life, since the personality remains in its immediacy:

it is the last conception of aesthetic life, since in a certain sense it has received within itself the consciousness of its own nullity.[1]

The distinction made by the author is clear. We are no longer faced with the dandy, the D'Annunzio-like aesthete who enjoys life and for whom every experience is but a poetic cue placed at the service of his own refined pursuit of pleasure. "The aestheticizing ideal [...], morbidly crepuscular, decadent and antisocial in its pseudo-heroic myth[2]" is surpassed in Kierkegaard by the sublime profile of an ultimate aesthete. He who lies on the highest step of the aesthetic stage, one step away from, but not yet part of, the ethical one. The despairing aesthete is fully aware of himself and the essence of one's life and is therefore destined to be forever miserable. He has opened his astounded eyes to the world; he was the first who dared to peer into the abyss by lifting its consoling and illusory Apollonian lid. The sight of the chilling and ill-concealed reality pierced him like Medusa's gaze, petrifying its scrutinizer; the truth, too heavy for his frail shoulders, terrifies him with the lucid force of disillusionment. Kierkegaard himself, in the aphorism of the *Journals* that would have most appealed to Nietzsche and Schopenhauer, writes that "Men are, by nature, more afraid of truth than death" (XI, A 352). Unequal and perpetually doomed to failure is man's struggle against the inexplicable cruelty of the world; just as vain will be his attempt to come to terms with it.

The sweet, sorrowful sigh of the lyrical self is moving but futile, a breath of rage in the wind that leads to a disarmed surrender. If the ordinary aesthete had put everything at stake, the very purpose of his life, on something transient, and destined to fade away, the despairing one has already understood the futility of everything and its ephemeral character. The former curses himself for the death of a coveted object, something tangible, precise, but if such an object could be replaced, he would be content and happy. With his gaze, the latter has penetrated the vanity of the world, the "solid nothingness[3]" that makes up reality and its insubstantiality.

---

[1] S. Kierkegaard, *Aut-Aut*, op. cit. p. 48.

[2] R. Cantoni, *Kierkegaard e la vita etica*, "Aut-Aut," op. cit., p. XIX.

[3] "I was frightened to find myself in the midst of nothingness, a nothingness myself. I felt like suffocating considering and feeling that everything is nothing, solid nothing" (G. Leopardi, *Zibaldone*, [85], Mondadori, Milano 1997, p. 120).

You still have in your power all the conditions for an aesthetic life, you have substance, you are independent, your health is perfect, your spirit is luxuriant, and you have not yet suffered because a maiden would not love you. Yet you are in despair. It is not an actual despair, for something real, but a potential despair, for every possibility in life. Your thought has anticipated life, you have penetrated the vanity of everything, but you have come no farther.[4]

There is therefore no remedy for his illness, no object can soothe his pain since he is already beyond it. Far from everything and estranged to himself, the despairing aesthete becomes a privileged spectator of a world that doesn't belong to him. Once he has learned the *vanitas vanitatum* of everything around him, he has nothing left to do but take refuge in his own nihilism; he has now ventured beyond the fleeting and illusory realm of sensitivity. He has ceased to chase after his own desire; no veil of Maya can now rescue him from the tragic reality. Nor will any divinatory wand be able to appease his disenchantment, for he needs nothing, or rather because he longs for nothingness. In his unfulfilling fantasies the despairing aesthete has experienced the futility of everything and now marches irrevocably toward the abyss. In an autobiographical passage of adamantine perfection, Giacomo Leopardi perfectly described the state of mind of the despairing man.

If I went mad right now, I believe that my madness would be to sit always with astonished eyes, with my mouth open, with my hands between my knees, without either laughing or crying, nor moving other than by force from the place where I was. I no longer had the energy to conceive any desire, nor even of death, not because I fear it on any account, but I see no more difference, between death and this life of mine, where not even sorrow comes to console me. This is the first time that boredom not only oppresses and tires me, but labors and tears me apart as a most grievous grief; and I am so afraid of the vanity of all things, and of the condition of men, once all passions are dead, as they are extinguished in my soul, that I lose myself completely, considering that even my despair is nothing.[5]

Self-annihilation and nullification are the inevitable punishment for those who have dared to look too far with baleful foresight. This is the

[4] S. Kierkegaard, *Aut-Aut*, op. cit. p. 48.
[5] Leopardi, quoted in R. Damiani, *All'apparir del vero*, Mondadori, Milano 1998, p. 141.

despairing aesthete's blessing and his curse; his superior sensitivity has made him at once extraordinarily capable and inconsolable, as the pioneer of the deepest sorrow. What Wilhelm reproaches his aesthete friend for is not being able to overcome his own silent abjection, thus making that quality leap that would ferry him to the ethical stage. Prisoner of his own despair, powerless in the face of his own resentment, the despairing aesthete is incapable of discerning in himself the "eternal value" constitutive of the ethical individual. Indeed, the aesthete is unable to willingly take upon himself his own despair unconditionally, and it is precisely this chronic inability to live passionately that prevents the aesthete from living ethically.

> And it is very sad, when one considers the life of men, that so many spend all their lives in quiet perdition. They cease to live before the end of their lives, not in the sense that the content of their life further evolves, and that is then possessed in this evolution, but they end up living almost outside themselves, they disappear like shadows, their immortal soul is dissipated, and they are not concerned about the question of its immortality, for they are already dissolved before they die. [...] Those who live aesthetically cannot give any satisfactory explanation about life, because they always live merely in the moment, and have solely a relative and limited consciousness of themselves [...] You detest all life's activities; very well; because in order for it to have any meaning, life must have continuity, which is lacking from yours.[6]

Wilhelm sees in his friend the superior but sterile sensitivity of he who has managed to identify the door that leads to the ethical stage but lacked the strength and courage to enter it. Paradoxically, what we are presented here is the personification of an aesthete who is not despairing *enough*, one who too soon lowered his gaze from the world with resignation, thus surrendering his own recondite, absolute value prematurely. Only the unconditional choice of despair can save him because true despair transcends all finitude and reveals that which is eternal and imperishable within us.

Kierkegaard introduces here one of his fundamental philosophical determinations, that of choice, which the present essay seeks to focus on. For Kierkegaard, every authentic choice of life or alternative of existence stems from an ethical decision, or rather, the choice itself is ethics. Total

---

[6] S. Kierkegaard, *Aut-Aut*, op. cit., pp. 17, 29, 50.

and totalizing deliberation is thus the necessary gateway to ethical life. It has been seen how every choice inevitably involves discarding one option in favor of another; even such a resolution can, however, be traced directly to a great original choice that determines the horizon of our existence, namely, the choice to choose.

> But what am I separating with my either/or? The good and the bad? No! I just want to lead you to the point where this choice will acquire real meaning for you. Everything revolves around it. When you have succeeded in taking someone to a crossroad, so that there is no other option for him than to choose, then he chooses right. [When] the time to choose has come, throw away all the rest, without care, you have lost nothing; but you choose.[7]

Anyone who is outside this determination (like the seducer or the despairing aesthete friend) lives in aesthetic indifference, a kind of chronic apathy of he who amuses himself with endless illusory possibilities without ever translating them into reality. Lost in the fantastic, the poet-aesthete is in danger of dying of loneliness and inactivity; he is the champion of reflection, but his plans never materialize, for such imaginative reveries occur only in thought. The ethical man is the author of an absolute, fundamental choice, having already chosen at the outset what criterion will govern the perspective of his life. The aesthete, on the other hand, loses himself, hesitates with indecision, and procrastinates the moment of choice indefinitely, thus letting others decide for him. He who lives in aesthetic indifference shuns from the absolute choice and "lives always and exclusively in the moment, his life unravels in an incoherent series of episodes that he is unable to explain."[8] Remo Cantoni writes:

> Nothing is more terrible than this dissolution of personality. At first, personality plays with possibilities, but then possibilities play with it, and we end up deprived of what is sacred and most intimate in the soul: the centralizing force of personality. [...] In this dispersion, in this psychic fragmentation, the aesthete believes that he is living the most splendid and sweetest of existences, which allows him to savor all the gifts and goods of life, without ever committing himself fully, always leaving a glimmer open to a new possibility. Ethics intends to divert man from the distraction of the manifold and the finite, and to let him access the infinite unity of personality,

---

[7] Ibid., p. 16.
[8] Kierkegaard, *Aut-Aut*, op. cit. p. 30.

[thus persuading him] that the meaning of life cannot consist in the finite, but in a higher calling.[9]

The essential characteristic of moral life is continuity, repetition, devoting one's life to the pursuit of a goal with commitment, earnestness, and constant dedication. "It is easy enough to make extemporaneous resolutions; what is arduous is to maintain them, not to submit to temptation, to discouragement, to make virtue the norm and habitual state of our character."[10] But how is the conversion from aesthetics to ethics possible? How does one make the transition from personality dispersed in the finite to personality concentrated in its spiritual value?

We have seen how Wilhelm identifies in despair the first, inescapable step toward the ethical stage, for it is only in despair—albeit a despair deeply and intensely coveted—that the self can become aware of itself and its possibility of transcending.

> To become conscious of the eternal significance of one's existence, one must despair. Nothing finite, not the whole world, can satisfy a soul where the yearning for the eternal is awakened. The only way to find the immortal spirit living in man is through despair. Despair requires strength, commitment, and concentration. Those who do not know despair do not know the meaning of life, no matter how many joys they experienced. One must despair wholeheartedly, soulfully, with all his strength. He who despairs finds the eternal man, he who throws himself into the sea of desperation finds the absolute. One must choose despair, and that is to choose oneself, not in one's immediacy, but in the eternal meaning of one's personality.[11]

Cantoni highlights the qualitative, ontological character of the process that leads individuals to despair.

> It is peculiar how for Kierkegaard, and for existentialism in general, the conversion to a higher stage of life does not occur through a call to rationality, to reflection, rather through an emotional call to one's inner self. Thought doubts but personality despairs, and despair is far more radical and profound than doubt. Despair is *totaliter* while doubt is only *partialiter*, because desperation encompasses the entire personality, while doubt can only seize thought. Intellectualism assimilates the value of personality in

[9] R. Cantoni, *Kierkegaard e la vita etica*, op. cit. pp. VI, VII.
[10] Ibid., p. X.
[11] Ibid.

thought and knows no other criteria outside of intelligence. But the real path toward the absolute is not the doubt generated by thought, to which only a few aristocratic spirits can aspire to, but total despair, in which even the most insignificant man can be immersed. [...] It is Saint Augustine's call to interiority, to recollection, in which is truth.[12]

In despair, the individual becomes aware of himself, of his own freedom, and of the possibilities that this awareness entails. The process of self-consciousness reveals to man his true self; he now discovers himself as "spirit," that is, as a way of being and placing himself in the world and relating to his body and soul. Making his own the Socratic maxim γνῶθι σεαυτόν, the "I" looks within himself as never before by configuring himself precisely as "a relation that relates to itself." He then lucidly discerns his own visceral matrix, takes note of his own fragmentary and conflicting nature, and realizes himself as a synthesis, that is, a set of opposing principles (finite/infinite, necessity/freedom, giveness/transcendence), which are mutually conflicting and irreconcilable, to finally become aware of his own absoluteness. His is a critical consciousness to the nth degree that will lead him to a condition of complete transparency and lucidity, which existentialists call *authenticity*.

[12] Ibid.

CHAPTER 3

The Choice of Self

Abstract The chapter sheds light on the process of choosing oneself as part of modern ethics. This is described by Kierkegaard as the synthesis of opposites within oneself (finite and infinite, relative and absolute, freedom and necessity, etc.), and the acknowledgment of one's absolute value that stems from it.

Keywords Kierkegaard • Freedom • Choice • Ethics • Absolute • Value • Synthesis • Giveness

The process that leads man to become aware of his own freedom and the nature of his self as a synthesis is far from easy and involves that work on oneself, based on a constant and painstaking exercise in self-perfection, on which modern ethics is founded; it is divided by Kierkegaard into three moments.

1. Self-recognition as absolute freedom;
2. Self-recognition as a necessity, based on one's history and conditioning;
3. Self-recognition in one's eternal worth through repentance.

The first phase, exaggerating the concept of freedom from antiquity as self-determination and autarky, outlines an absolute, unconditioned, and

© The Author(s), under exclusive license to Springer Nature Switzerland AG 2023
R. Pugliese, *The Dizziness of Freedom in Kierkegaard and Sartre*, https://doi.org/10.1007/978-3-031-38138-6_3

de-situated freedom. Drunk with his own power, the free man believes he has the world at his feet; he lives in an abstraction, what he sees all around him is but a deceptive reflection of the unquenchable flame of his concupiscence. He experiences the drama of he who discovers a haven of stillness in his mind where he can be God, king of his thoughts with his eyes closed, but in this reality he has himself as his only subject. The second phase presents man with his limits. The freedom of the self, from creative becomes now creaturely, from absolute, situated. Man clashes against the limits of his contingency and discovers that he has a history, and that this history is indivisibly interwoven with the histories of other men, bound to become a single, collective history. This is the concept which Sartre will name "giveness," and that is the recognition by a particular individual as having been born in a certain place, at a certain time, to specific parents, with unique psycho-physical characteristics, and within a well-defined social context. He admits to being part of a species and understands his inalienable ties. This whole complex framework of familial, affective, psychological, political, geographical, historical, and cultural conditioning means that even choices that man thought were his own and conceived in complete self-autonomy are in fact not his at all. This downsizing from an active stage of indeterminate, absolute possibility to a passive stage of binding and constrained necessity, seems to confine man within the shackles of his own finiteness.

The awareness that one constitutes a derived synthesis, posited by others, and to be a product of history in continuity with the species, risks clipping the wings of the individual's flight toward his absoluteness. For Kierkegaard, on the other hand, this is the only way to reach one's own eternal value, the ultimate embrace with the absolute, as Jean Wahl writes, "Par l'existence à la transcendance. Par le défilé où je ne puis passer que seul, vers la hauteur qui domine tout."[1] Like any other decisive turning point in Kierkegaard's thought, this passage through the gateway to eternity comes at a price. The element of "repentance" comes into play here, without which no authentic transformation can subsist. For the Danish philosopher, in fact, there can be no redemption without true suffering, nor atonement without inner grievance. The individual who has recognized and realized himself first as absolute freedom (as a desiring entity,

---

[1] "From existence to transcendence. Through the cleft where I can only pass alone, to the height that dominates all" (J. Wahl, *Études Kierkegaardiennes*, Librairie Philosophique J. Vrin, Paris 1967, p. 265).

aspiring to something), later as a necessity (and, as such, determined, finite), now has to repent, that is, to take lucidly and with full responsibility his own background of conditions and bonds upon himself, thus redeeming it in its entirety and complexity. It is a painful process intended to dig into the depths of the individual to shed light on the conditionings related to upbringing, childhood, era, and society; a compass-less journey into the darkness of the Freudian *Id*, to plumb the innermost folds of the self. The process of psychoanalysis is aimed precisely at the recovery and realization of one's ideal self, at the divine within us, and at a newfound harmony between self and world. Kierkegaard dedicates unforgettable pages of *Either/Or* to this theme, where he describes the discovery and choosing oneself and one's inner essence in the manner of a mystical rebirth.

> So I fight for freedom, [...] for the future, for the either/or. This is the treasure I intend to leave to those I love in the world. If my little son were now in the age of being able to understand me and my last hour had come, I would say to him: I leave you neither titles nor honors; but I know where lies a treasure that can make you richer than anything in the world, and this treasure belongs to you and for it you do not have to thank me, because I do not want your spirit to have to suffer in owing everything to someone: this treasure is buried within you, it is an either/or that makes men greater than angels. [...] When all is silence around us, everything is as solemn as a night full of stars, when the soul is alone in the midst of the world, in front of it appears not a distinguished man, but the eternal power itself, the sky almost opens wide, and the self chooses itself or rather receives itself. In that instant the soul has seen the supreme height, that which no mortal eye can see and what will never be forgotten, personality receives the knight's banner, which ennobles it for eternity. Man does not become different from what he was before, he just becomes himself; consciousness gathers, and he is himself. Just as an heir, even if he were heir to all the riches of this world, does not possess them before coming of age, so the richest personality is nothing before it has chosen itself, and, on the other hand, even what we might call the most miserable personality is everything when it has chosen itself. For greatness does not consist in being this or that, but in being oneself, and this anyone can do if he wishes.[2]

It has been shown how the man who aims to find himself moves from aesthetic despair to later become aware of his freedom and the threefold

---

[2] S. Kierkegaard, *Aut-Aut*, op. cit. p. 26–27.

nature of his self as a synthesis. Freedom and self-awareness are therefore the foundational traits of the ethical man. The former configures him as pure and unlimited possibility, the second makes him a limited being conditioned by its own inescapable reality. The individual now has to take the last and most difficult leap toward the absolute self. This can only come about through repentance, that is, through the rekindling of the terrible inheritance within us, which loses us and which, only at the end of a terrible ride suspended on the edge of the abyss, will restore us to ourselves. Of capital importance in this journey is the choice of the abyss, to be willing to dive headfirst into the unknown, to be ready for a total sacrifice in order to come out later profoundly renewed. Dostoevsky described this state of mind perfectly, although the despair of his characters rarely leads to authentic redemption:

> His condition at that moment resembled the condition of a man standing on a frightening precipice, as the earth opens up beneath him and already landslides, already shudders for the last time, collapses, drags him into the abyss, and meanwhile the unhappy man no longer has either the strength or the steadiness of mind to leap back, to avert his eyes from the gaping abyss; the abyss attracts him and he finally dives into it, hastening the moment of his own doom.[3]

Without sacrifice, the individual is pinned down to being a mere product of contingent factors, thus best declining Auguste Comte's paradox "The living are ruled by the dead."[4] Instead, it is necessary first to understand oneself and then to choose oneself fully, to take upon oneself our history, and to decide to carry its burden alone. Without this backward process, freedom itself is destined to remain an illusion.

---

[3] F. Dostoevsky, *Il sosia*, Rizzoli, Milano 1998, p. 64.

[4] Are the living then governed by the dead?—Jacques Maritain asked himself this, taking up a statement of Comte's. In his opinion, the positivist philosopher would not have understood the terrifying aspect of the statement, grasped instead by Kierkegaard, and answered thus, "All the dead buried in my inheritance weigh in me on my destiny, their dreams and their poisons fermenting in me are the hidden evil that distresses me. For in every hereditary ancestry there is a particular imbalance and disorder which, to the extent that the determinism of matter is at stake, inexorably drives the unfortunate living person toward the abyss. Only at the extreme point of this cursed ride are there, in his immortal soul, free will and grace as the only possibility of liberation and of one day coming into possession of his true name and true self" (J. Maritain, *La filosofia morale. Esame storico e critico dei grandi sistemi*, Morcelliana, Brescia 1988, p. 417).

The category of repentance, however, is not and cannot be projected only to the past but must also encompass the future. It is the willingness to change that makes one free, that which removes the individual from the inert crystallization of past events, and places him or her in the broader prospect of the future. Freedom is, therefore, also congruity of means to an end, the gauging of one's abilities and resources in view of a definite life project. That is why the attainment of the ideal self is different for each person. Free, then, is he who knows what he can become and what he must become, without betraying himself, and indulging in one's nature. The redemption of what is divine within us, the return to the ego's original contact with the *icona dei*, involves working on oneself until one becomes the best possible version of oneself, and none other. Such is the ultimate scope of the ethical man, namely, the ego's commitment to become what he is, what he wants, what he can, and what he must. He moves from his own immediacy and spontaneity to realize himself as a moral, eternal, inwardly purified, and renewed individual. His journey to find himself is a renaissance, or rather a transfiguration. The concepts of freedom and becoming act as a link between being-in-itself and the moral self.[5]

And it would nevertheless be wrong to believe that such a transformation can easily be achieved, so to speak, from the outside, through a meticulous but sterile emulation of others' behavior. The regeneration of the individual occurs only as a result of an entirely inner, troubled, and hidden journey, a "running in place" that leads him from his concretion (what is innate and natural within him), to the tangency with the divine (the best version of himself). Such will be the meaning of what Sartre calls *project*. The discovery of the self must be personal, laborious, and authentic, hence not transferable. And all the while man is always fully responsible for himself and in front of himself as he produces that existential harmony, which is given by the symmetry of the different parts of his personality. Ethics is this: construction, work, *Bildung*, choice and commitment on self, harmonious development, and perfect balance between our characteristics, talents, and abilities, that is, between our many possible selves. Throughout all of this, our constant fixed point, the supreme and indispensable reference, the point of both departure and arrival, is the "I." The "I" accompanies us throughout the entire journey, like the wayfarer's shadow.

---

[5] J. Wahl, *Études Kierkegaardiennes*, op. cit. pp. 257–269.

Kierkegaard rejects the consoling conciliatory synthesis of G.W.F. Hegel's dialectic identifiable with the Danish expression *Baage-Og*, meaning both ... and ..., *et* ... *et* ..., in favor of his famous *Enten-Eller*, i.e., either ... or ..., *aut* ... *aut* ..., paradigm of his conception of choice and, significantly, the title of one of his major works. The Kierkegaardian formulation of the three different stages of existence (aesthetic, ethical, and religious), as well as his conception of leap and infinite qualitative difference between them, is posited as a function of this problem.

Indeed, every choice also inevitably implies renunciation. The gap between the opposing alternatives of existence thus becomes unbridgeable and threatening, the presence of nothingness (what may not be or may not happen within each choice) reveals its terrifying face to man, annihilating him. The unbearable weight of the distressing "sense of possibility"[6] throws man into a state of perpetual fear and trembling. He suffers from this unconditional freedom and needs a necessity to provide him with direction and guidance.

> For in the decisions concerning the spirit one can resolve freely and venture, but in relation to finiteness one must in the end be constrained. Finite decisions are a too little thing for infinity to reach them—so one must be compelled. Being constrained is finitude's only resource. The choice of freedom, the only thing that saves in the sphere of infinity![7]

The painful and melancholic irreconcilability between opposite life paths was rendered masterfully by American poet Robert Frost in *The Road Not Taken* (1916).

> Two roads diverged in a yellow wood,
> And sorry I could not travel both
> And be one traveler, long I stood
> And looked down one as far as I could
> To where it bent in the undergrowth;
> Then took the other, as just as fair,
> And having perhaps the better claim,
> Because it was grassy and wanted wear;
> Though as for that the passing there

---

[6] S. Kierkegaard, *Il concetto dell'angoscia*, Sansoni, Firenze 1965, p. 54.
[7] S. Kierkegaard, *Diario*, op. cit., [1179].

Had worn them really about the same,
And both that morning equally lay
In leaves no step had trodden black.
Oh, I kept the first for another day!
Yet knowing how way leads on to way,
I doubted if I should ever come back.
I shall be telling this with a sigh
Somewhere ages and ages hence:
Two roads diverged in a wood, and I—
I took the one less traveled by,
And that has made all the difference.

The alternatives of existence, Frost tells us, are not just irreconcilable and opposite (1–3), but almost indistinguishable. The traveler on the path of life pauses at length to contemplate them, noting their substantial sameness but finally and resolutely chooses only one, "the one least traveled by" (3–12). It is difficult to say which is the triggering factor or foothold safe to cling to and that makes man lean toward a given direction over another. All he has left with is a vague impression or ephemeral inclination within a decision-making framework that appears as uncertain and foggy as ever. Man chooses in the dark, in the abyss of existential choice there is no compass or pole star to guide him by pointing him north. And, nevertheless, to live is to choose, and he cannot hold back too long from the impulse toward a path of life, whether it be the path for the individual to shape himself and grow, or a supreme principle around which to organize every decision, as Frost seems to suggest.

Still, the choice of one path over another does not occur without bringing with it an infinite melancholy and nostalgia (these themes are near and dear to Romantic authors) for the impossibility of returning (nostalgia means precisely suffering for the νόστος, which is ancient Greek for "return"), for what could have been and never will be (13–17). The traveler knows that he is faced with an insoluble dilemma. Choosing one path will forever exclude the other; it is impossible to walk them both, just as it will be impossible one day to return to the road not taken. Any decision is, consequently, permanent. The irreversibility of each and every choice looms inescapably over man and on any experience or situation where he comes to find himself. The unbreakable bond between the experience of reality and such determination (irreversibility, the impossibility of turning back) compels him to always come to terms with it, regardless of the magnitude of the situation in which he finds himself. Thus, there is no qualitative difference between "leading peoples" and "getting drunk in solitude," since each choice conditions us irreversibly.

The looming of nothingness over being and choice, and the presence of terrible and annihilating possibilities that await man at the gate of his every decision will be concepts that all modern existentialism will inherit and make its own. The thinker, however, who will elaborate most thoroughly and effectively the concept of freedom and what it entails will be Sartre.[8] In *Existentialism Is a Humanism* (1946), he invites us to look into ourselves with lucidity, and to become responsible (a key word in Sartre) for all our behavior, taking note of its uniqueness and irrevocability. It is Sartre himself, as we shall see, who stresses the necessity to come to terms with the consequences that every action, even the most seemingly insignificant, entails.

---

[8] Sartre is decisive for the invention of the philosophical category of responsibility. It will later be seen how, while starting from distinctive Kierkegaardian premises, the French philosopher takes his reflections on freedom, the life project and transcendence to new heights.

CHAPTER 4

Existentialism and the Birth of the Modern Era

Abstract The chapter aims to provide a brief overview of existentialism as well as its contribution to modern philosophy. The rise of modern science, the decline of rationalism, and the critique of academic philosophies are all indicated as decisive factors in the advent of existentialism within the context of "The Age of Anxiety" in Europe (1918–1939).

Keywords Existentialism • Anxiety • Science • Weber • Rationalism • Pascal • Alienation • Absurdity

More than 80 years have passed since existentialism first exploded onto the European intellectual scene, creating a veritable cultural revolution in fields such as psychoanalysis, literature, art, theater, and cinema. Before long, concepts such as anguish, alienation, and absurdity came to assert themselves, disrupting the common thinking of the time. Existentialism was the product of the complex political, economic, and social crisis framework of the early postwar period.

Known as "The Age of Anxiety," the period 1918–1939 was marked by a series of artistic manifestations, cultural trends, and achievements in science destined to shake the social consciousness of the time to its core.[1]

[1] See R. May, *The Meaning of Anxiety*, Hauraki Publishing, San Francisco, California 2015.

The fear of modernity, the collapse of social progress and optimism, the celebration of the irrational side of the human mind and the absurdity of existence, the critique of traditional science and Comtian positivism, and the undoing of Hegelian idealism, were just some of the themes that the new cultural season, represented by the work of Stravinsky, Freud, Kafka, Breton, Einstein, Heidegger, and Sartre—to name but a few—had brought to light. Against such a tumultuous backdrop, existentialism established itself with rare power, leaving a deep echo in the decades to come. Whatever opinion one has today about the early postwar phenomenon called existentialism, it is difficult to ignore the significant philosophical contribution of its protagonists (first and foremost Heidegger and Sartre) and precursors (Nietzsche and, above all, Kierkegaard). This new worldview was strongly influenced by the emergence on the European scene of modern science and the new view of reality connected with it. Sociologist Max Weber has called this turn "the disenchantment of the world."[2] The modern age enshrines the primacy of consciousness over all other faculties, contributing to initiate in Europe a process of rationalization that will dismantle all the theological or metaphysical premises on which universal value judgments had previously been based. Man no longer harbors any illusions about the reality of his ideals, much less the positivist illusion that such ideals can be objectively grounded in historical or social facts and their development.[3]

> From this emerges in any case the absurdity of the conviction—which sometimes prevails even among the historians of our discipline—that it can be the aim, however distant, of the sciences of culture to work out a closed system of concepts, within the framework of which reality can be enclosed in an artificer in any sense definitive, and from which it is then deduced.[4]

According to Weber, pre-modern societies conceived of the world as an "enchanted garden," where nature is thought of as a system ordered according to precise values and that determines in advance the specific

---

[2] C. Guignon, D. Pereboom, *Existentialism—Basic writings,* Hackett Publishing Company, Indianapolis/Cambridge 2001, p. XIV.

[3] "*Culture* is a finite section of the meaningless infinity of the world's becoming, to which is attributed meaning and significance from the human point of view" (M. Weber, *Il metodo delle scienze storico-sociali,* Einaudi, Torino 2003, p. 96).

[4] M. Weber, *Il metodo delle scienze storico-sociali,* op. cit. p. 100.

function and purpose of each entity. The ancient Greeks, for example, believed in a rational structure governing the real, in a teleologically ordered κόσμος, that is, based on a finalistic conception of the world where the concept of justice is equivalent to the perfect exercise by every entity of its proper function. In the Middle Ages such a view is replaced by the presence of God as the guarantor of every principle; man's supreme purpose then becomes that of realizing the divine plan, according to a predetermined project. Later in the Renaissance, reality is conceived of as a chain of entities, where, not unlike the Greek concept, each being assumes a precise role and is linked to the surrounding world through a series of relationships.

The advent of modern science in the seventeenth century irreparably compromised this idea of the world as a cozy and familiar place, forever dispossessing it of meaning and significance. Thanks to this new perspective, even the universe is objectified, and regarded as a vast aggregate of particles devoid of purpose and value. Man loses his central position in the universe and now finds himself relegated to a small planet at the edge of an unknown universe among billions of galaxies. The proto-existentialist philosopher Blaise Pascal, perfectly captured the sense of bewilderment and loneliness originated by the new scientific discoveries and especially the Copernican revolution, when, in the section of *Pensées* (1669) significantly titled "Man without God," he writes "The eternal silence of those infinite spaces terrifies me."[5]

> When I consider the short duration of my life, absorbed in the eternity that precedes and follows it, and the small space that I occupy and even see, sunk in the infinite immensity of the spaces that I do not know and that do not know me, I am frightened and amazed to find myself here rather than there, for there is no reason for me to be here rather than there, now rather than later. Who put me here? By whose order and authority has this place and time been destined for me?[6]

> Let man therefore contemplate the entirety of nature in its high and full majesty; let him turn his gaze away from the petty objects that surround him. Let him gaze upon that blazing light, arranged like an eternal lamp to re-lighten the universe; let the earth appear to him as a dot in comparison

[5] B. Pascal, *Pensieri*, Rizzoli, Milano 2016, [119].
[6] Ibid., [118].

with the vast circle which that star describes, and let him be astonished that
this same vast circle is but an insignificant stretch in comparison with that
which the rotating stars in the firmament embrace. [...] All this visible world
is but an imperceptible point within the vast bosom of nature. No idea
approaches it. We inflate our conceptions beyond imaginable spaces: we give
birth only to atoms in comparison with the reality of things. It is an infinite
sphere in which the center is everywhere, the circumference nowhere. [...]
Let man, returning to himself, consider what he is in comparison with what
exists; let him consider himself as lost in this remote corner of nature; and,
from this narrow cell in which he finds himself, I mean the universe, let him
learn to estimate in the right way the earth, the realms the cities and himself.
What is a man in the infinite? [...] For finally what is man in nature? A
nothing compared to the infinite, a whole in comparison with nothingness,
a middle ground between nothingness and the whole. Infinitely far from
understanding these extremes, the end of things and their beginning are for
him invincibly concealed in an impenetrable secret; equally unable to see the
nothingness from which he is drawn, and the infinity by which he is
swallowed up. [...] This is our true condition. It prevents us from knowing
with certainty and ignoring absolutely. We sail in a vast sea, always uncertain
and fluctuating, driven from one extreme to another. Every term at which
we think to dock and stop falters and abandons us, and if we follow it it
escapes our grasp, slips from our hands, and drifts away in an eternal flight.
Nothing stops for us. It is the natural condition for us, and yet the most
contrary to our tendencies. We burn with the desire to find a stable ground,
and an ultimate secure base to build a tower that rises to infinity; but our
foundations crumble, and the earth opens up to the abyss.[7]

Existentialist thought would take its starting point from this feeling of
desolation and estrangement from life only to later turn out to be critical
of the scientific progress behind it. This new worldview was accompanied
by the emergence of new centralized states and the idea of the individual
as a clearly distinct entity opposed to society as a whole. Previously, the
identity of the individual was defined in relation to the role and function
he occupied in the community of which he was a part. Such a scenario
seemed to leave no room for the concept of the individual understood in
the modern sense as a unique entity, individuated and independent from
others. On the contrary, a person was primarily defined by his or her place
within the network of social and familial relationships.

---

[7] Ibid., [43].

In the modern view, the way the individual relates to society is profoundly and painfully different. As the season of certainty has waned, he
finds himself trapped and in constant struggle against an impersonal and
dehumanizing society; the distance between man and the world becomes
increasingly unbridgeable, fueling the sense of isolation and alienation
that will culminate in the contemporary age.

Friedrich Nietzsche conveyed the deep and irreversible crisis of
traditional values in the words "God is dead." The expression marks with
exalted focus the collapse of the concept of the absolute, in all its forms,
and the destruction of any certainty or metaphysical consolation in the
Western world. Ideas concerning the transcendence of values, whether
embodied in the κόσμος of the ancient Greeks, the God of Christianity, the
Humanism and reason of the Enlightenment, or superstructures such as
history, morality, religion, and society, are now revealed as what they are;
nothing more than human constructs, artificially created over the centuries
and transmitted over generations to survive and give meaning and purpose
to an existence otherwise emptied of all meaning. The complex human
castle of phony absolutes and "millennial lies" is nevertheless doomed to
collapse since it appeals to reasons, justifications, and more generally to a
meaning that is not traced in this life. And where the old traditional system
has failed, no new system seems ready to take over. For Nietzsche, the lack
of absolutes is what is most terrifying in this scenario. Man's realization of
the absence of justifications and solid reasons hitherto taken for granted in
Western civilization will therefore have only one outcome: nihilism, the
complete undoing of all values.

Existentialists move precisely from these premises. The death of God
represents the landslide, beneath our feet, of the ground that legitimizes
our existence and defines the purpose of our lives. Man finds himself
abandoned, forgotten, thrown into a world without motivation or
direction, a world deaf to his desperate call. Despite his vain clinging to
society for comfort and protection, he ultimately finds himself irretrievably
alone, an isolated individual who will have to find the content and meaning
of his life in himself. Anxiety, distress, nausea, and shipwreck are the terms
that define man's existential condition, his struggle with a hostile and
foreign world, deprived of purpose and design. What such formulations
are meant to suggest is that there is no fixed and unchanging foundation
for our beliefs and convictions, no predetermined essences to guide us in

our choices, just as any sense of predestination that ascribes specific function and value to us is absent. Existentialist doctrine, however, will be able to go far beyond the recognition of the contemporary age's lack of absolutes, also overcoming the sense of bewilderment induced by the vertigo of freedom. Unlike Nietzsche and Schopenhauer therefore, nihilism will be for the existentialists primarily a starting point, a necessary premise from which to build, rather than an autonomous and self-concluded moment of their reflection.

CHAPTER 5

Human Existence

Abstract The chapter tackles the problem of human existence in existentialism. By focusing on the—intrinsically human—subjective experience of thinking and feeling, existentialist philosophers set out to explore issues related to the meaning and purpose of life. Man is a synthesis of infinite and finite, situation and action, freedom and necessity. As such, man must transcend the conflictual nature of his condition to claim his freedom and realize himself in his eternal value.

Keywords Existentialism • Transcendence • Hegel • Jaspers • Sartre • Heidegger • Essence • Project

In an attempt to explain the condition of man in the modern age, existentialists formulated a new conception of human existence. In open controversy with what had been the philosophical tradition until then, and its endeavor to understand and study man as an object (whether it be mind, body, or a combination of the two), the existentialists have characterized human existence as struggle, conflict, and eternal tension between opposing elements. In *The Philosophy of Existence* (1938), Karl Jaspers identifies in the synergy philosophy/science the answer to the contemporary spiritual crisis, as well as the complete realization of pro-existentialist thought as such:

© The Author(s), under exclusive license to Springer Nature
Switzerland AG 2023
R. Pugliese, *The Dizziness of Freedom in Kierkegaard and Sartre*,
https://doi.org/10.1007/978-3-031-38138-6_5

This bewilderment of reality, despite the accentuation of realism in our epoch, a bewilderment from which, as soon as we became aware of it, arose the new spiritual anxiety and the new direction of philosophical thought, we do not consider it in its totality: instead, we shall attempt to point out the intricate historical process of this return to reality, a return that took place in many different forms, considering our relationship to science as a concrete and essential motif of this theme.[1]

Specifically, it is the leap between immanence and transcendence that is the viaticum for the realization of being and freedom.

This is the leap that marks the transition from all that is temporally experience-able [...] to Being itself, which is real and eternal. [...] This leap marks the passage from the infinite comprehensiveness that we are, as determinate being, consciousness, spirit, to the infinite comprehensiveness that we recognize as the world, to the infinite comprehensiveness that is Being itself.[2]

In the *Phenomenology of Spirit* (1807), Hegel distinguishes between two dimensions or aspects that make up the human being. On the one hand, humans are natural organisms, members of the animal kingdom, with needs and desires similar to those of other animals. On the other, they are profoundly different from other animals who merely follow immediate instincts and drives, dictated by their own natural condition; what they lack is the capacity to transcend their natural limits. The existence of awareness (or consciousness) is precisely what in human beings marks a qualitative difference from the order of other animals. As Hegel writes, conscience is precisely the notion of the self.[3] In other words, human beings as conscious beings are able to reflect and evaluate themselves in relation to their own nature. Consciousness enables us to distance ourselves from our immediate drives in order to analyze them rationally. Hegel describes this uniquely human capacity by saying that consciousness transcends its own limits, and, since these limits belong to it, consciousness transcends itself.[4]

---

[1] K. Jaspers, La *filosofia dell'esistenza*, Bompiani, Milano 1943, p. 17.
[2] Ibid., pp. 48–49.
[3] G.W.F. Hegel, *Fenomenologia dello spirito*, Einaudi, Torino 2008, p. 62.
[4] Ibid.

For Heidegger and Sartre, as for Jaspers, the concept of transcendence is precisely what makes human beings unique, for whom one's essence is constantly put into question. To be happy, man does not simply need to satisfy his instincts, for he also questions his own identity and reflects on the value of the things he desires. Being able to transcend the immediacy of basic needs and drives means being able to aspire to a higher level of ambitions, dreams, goals, and objectives. The ability to reflect on who we are involves being able to deny our appetitive-desiring component, to say *no* to our immediate inclinations. In doing so, we introduce a no, a nothingness, a subdued emptiness into the perfect *plenum* of the natural order. Denial and resistance provoke a rupture within the datum of man; this occurs through the precise decision on the part of the individual to interact with it in order to modify it and give it the desired direction actively, in the course of one's life.

> What I properly am never becomes my possession but remains my possibility of being. If I knew this, I would no longer be because in this temporal subsistence of mine I have consciousness of myself, only as a being denied and resolved. The truth of existence can thus rest in itself unconditionally, without wanting to know itself. This unreflected elementariness appears in higher existences, which never attain any image, any consciousness of their own essence.[5]

So a crack, a fissure, a nothingness is introduced within the fullness of being by human existence. Taking an initiative regarding oneself, being willing to modify one's own intrinsic nature, creates the perpetual possibility of an extended *no* to all that has been and is. In this way, according to Hegel, consciousness commits violence against itself[6] by opening a chink in the heart of being to an infinite and inexhaustible desire; the incessant need to fill the gap of being once and for all realizing that higher order of ideals and aspirations created by consciousness itself.[7] Human

[5] K. Jaspers, *La filosofia dell'esistenza*, op. cit. p. 65.

[6] G.W.F. Hegel, *Fenomenologia dello spirito*, op. cit. p. 62.

[7] Thus Sartre on the self-sufficient character of consciousness, which is therefore not to be conceived as an "already given" or as interior to the subject, but whose origin must always be located outside of it: "Consciousness becomes self-conscious insofar as it is conscious of a transcendent object [...] the object is in front of it with its characteristic capacity, but it is simply consciousness of being consciousness in this object. This is the law of its existence" (J.-P. Sartre, *La trascendenza dell'ego*, Marinotti Edizioni, Milano 2012, p. 34).

existence is experienced as lack, deprivation, as a chasm struggling to be filled; it is constantly agitated by desires and efforts to endorse one's immediate needs and impressions, and therefore, according to Hegel, can never find peace.

Hegel thus presents human existence as a tension between two aspects of the self: the in-itself—that is, our innate, finite, and empirical character—and the for-itself—that is, the reflective/speculative moment, which leads us to interpret and evaluate, thus transcending our mere giveness. Kierkegaard, playing with the complex Hegelian terminology, describes this relation inherent in human nature in *The Sickness unto Death*, writing that the self is "a relation that relates to itself."[8] Nietzsche emphasizes the duality of the self by saying that humans are both creatures and creators. Heidegger and Sartre later relate to man as a contraposition between immanence and transcendence (for Sartre essence and existence), finite and infinite, caducous and eternal, necessity and freedom, situation and action, *datum* and project.[9] For the former, human being (or *Dasein*, i.e., beingness understood as man's own mode of being in the world) is composed of concretion and freedom. As part of nature, Heidegger says, being/*Dasein* is abandoned, "thrown" into the world, stuck in it and despite itself absorbed by it because of its physicality. At the same time, *Dasein*, as transcendent being transcends nature. That is to say, "although *Dasein* remains anchored to nature because of its corporeality, [...] it is nevertheless in some way alien to its own nature by virtue of its transcendent character, that is, thanks to the fact that it is always and ultimately free."[10] For Sartre, too, man is essentially transcendence, freedom (understood precisely as transcendence from the given); transcendence is not a state or condition already inherent in us, rather something to strive for incessantly, a tension toward the infinite (in this equatable to the romantic concept of *Sehnsucht*, man's spasmodic yearning for the absolute), a yearning, the desire for freedom or rather the desire of desire.[11] Freedom is

[8] S. Kierkegaard, *Il concetto dell'angoscia-La malattia mortale*, Sansoni, Firenze 1973.

[9] In *Essere e avere* (1933) Gabriel Marcel formulates the ontological distinction between problem and mystery: "Problem and mystery are two distinct ways for human intelligence to relate cognitively to reality" (F. Riva, *Essere e avere di Marcel e il dibattito su esistenza ed essere nell'esistenzialismo*, Paravia, Torino 1990, pp. 89–90).

[10] M. Heidegger, *Metaphysical Foundations of Logic*, trans. Michael Heim, Indiana University Press, Bloomington, Indiana 1984, p. 166.

[11] "The existentialist will never take man as an end, because man is always to be made" (J.-P. Sartre, 80 *L'esistenzialismo è un umanismo*, Mursia, Milano 1946, p. 84).

action, tension, change, the relationship inherent in man between determination and transcendence. The relationship between self-determination and the absolute is explicated through the desire with which man is capable of overcoming the prison of his own giveness. By applying the definitions of absolute and relative, qualitative and quantitative in a metaphysical key, Henri Bergson sheds light on the irreducible relationship between intuition and analysis:

> In this sense, and in this sense alone, *absolute* is synonymous with *perfection*. All the photographs of a city, taken from all possible points of view, no matter how indefinitely they complement each other, will never equate that specimen in relief which is the city where one walks. All translations of a poem into all possible languages, no matter how many nuances they add to the nuances and, correcting each other with a kind of mutual retouching, give a most faithful image of the poem they translate, but they will never render the inner sense of the original. [...] But the absolute is perfect in the sense that it is perfectly what it is. [...] Seen from within, an absolute is, therefore, something simple; but seen from outside, that is, relative to something else, it becomes in relation to those signs that express it, the gold coin that will never run out of change. Now, that which lends itself at the same time to an indivisible apprehension and to an inexhaustible enumeration is, by definition, an infinite.[12]

Desire consists precisely of each person's original relationship between his own giveness and the absolute within him, and transcendence is the realization of one's ideality, the nostalgic attainment of something we lack and yearn for. Such transfiguration is possible because it defines the self as a reality that is failed, defective, and lacking. For Sartre, no man is a full and complete being, a Parmenidian *perfectus* always identical to himself as a geometric shape; instead, man is a "decompression of being,"[13] flawed and indefinable.

Hegel thought that the conscience's tension between our embodiment and our yearning for freedom could finally be resolved through a conciliatory dialectical process. Here is where the initial debt of existentialist

---

[12] H. Bergson, *Introduzione alla metafisica*, Laterza, Bari, 1970, pp. 44–45.

[13] "Man is constantly outside himself: only by projecting and losing himself outside himself does he make man exist, and, on the other hand, only by pursuing transcendent ends can he exist. [...] Not in turning towards himself, but always seeking outside himself a purpose—which is that liberation, that particular actualization—man will realize himself precisely as human" (J.-P. Sartre, *L'esistenzialismo è un umanismo*, op. cit., pp. 85–86).

philosophy toward Hegelian thought is finally extinguished to make way for an entirely new and far less consolatory worldview. For existentialists, in fact, such a resolution of the conflict turns out to be extremely difficult to achieve. As a living being capable of reflection, man will always be something more than a factual, situated entity, limited to his here-and-now condition, and consequently in his life there will always be a gap between what he is and what he might become. The core of existentialist reflection might be this: the conception of the self as a constant struggle rather than as an unchanging, predetermined entity carries with it the idea of ourselves as a continuous happening. What defines our identity as a person is not a particular set of permanent properties, rather the happening of our ceaseless becoming through which we struggle to find a resolution to the tension that defines our situation in the world. As perpetual happening, we are what we become throughout our entire lives.[14] This means that human existence has a definite temporal structure. Indeed, man does not persist unchanged in existence, occupying a definite place in the infinite series of *nows* of time. On the contrary, human existence is, so to speak, cumulative, (i.e. encompassing every single lived experience) and oriented according to criteria of direction and purpose, unlike the persistent presence of objects. The individual is inexorably driven by the desire to be something, to complete a part of himself, and to heal the crack in the core of his being. The result of such a drive (which existentialists call the "aspiration to be God") is to push man ever forward, toward the future, setting as his goal the realization of the fundamental plans that define his transcendence.[15]

At the same time, our past also plays a fundamental role in the economy of our existence because of the way it is thought about and interpreted in view of the future. We are beings deeply connected to time in the sense that our character of finality leads us to collect what has been and to shape and direct it as a resource in view of a plan. Our actions in the present are points of intersection between past and future since in each of them what has been is revealed for what will come to be. That is why for existentialism

---

[14] "Here I want, therefore, to recall the determination that in what precedes I gave of the ethical element: that by which man becomes what he becomes" (S. Kierkegaard, *Enten-Eller*, V, Adelphi, Milano 1989, p. 144).

[15] J.D. Wild, *Existentialism as a Philosophy*, in E. Kern, *Sartre: A Collection of Critical Essays*, Prentice-Hall, Englewood Cliffs (N.J., 1962); J. Macquarrie, *In Search of Humanity: A Theological and Philosophical Approach*, SCM Press, London 1982, pp. 10–24.

the concept of pure presence, that is, of an autonomous entity, untethered from past and future, cannot exist. The individual is constantly out there, always beyond his own determination as a mere entity in the present. The term to exist is thus to be understood, according to Heidegger, in a literal sense as *ex-sistere*, or ex-stand, that is, to stand outside pure presence, to go beyond the given reality in the direction of possibility. As Sartre also says, man is nothing but what he does of himself.[16] The cumulative, all-encompassing character of human existence implies that each of our actions contributes to the shaping of our life in its entirety. With each action, we are shaping the configuration of roles and traits that make up the course of our lives. Such is the identity we are assuming for ourselves. For existentialists, we are what we do as we live and actively determine ourselves. We are self-creating or self-shaping beings. We define our human reality through our choices, and in our relationship with the world.

Sartre in this regard affirms that man's existence is characterized by the space of the plan, by choice, and thus by the freedom and responsibility that derive from it, and he expresses this idea beautifully in the famous postulate "existence precedes essence." For the French philosopher in fact, there is no fixed essence in man that establishes a priori how he should live. Rather, each of us decides to shape our essence (the way we are in the world) through our actions and choices, in other words, through our existence. For Sartre, and for Heidegger before him, man's essence, his human reality is, in fact existence. Essence is normally understood, according to the philosophical tradition, as the set of determining characteristics of an entity, without which that entity would not be what it is; essence is thus synonymous with nature. For existentialists, on the other hand, the essence (or nature) of man is that he does not have a predetermined essence, that is, he cannot be distinguished from other entities by characteristics given once and for all.[17]

---

[16] W. Kaufmann, *Existentialism from Dostoevsky to Sartre*, New American Library, New York 1975, pp. 40–48.

[17] *The absence of beingness consists in its existence.* "The characters that will turn out to be proper to this being therefore have nothing to do with the simply-present 'properties' of a simply-present being, 'having the appearance' of being so or so, but are always and only possible manners of being of the being, and nothing else. [...] Hence the term beingness by which we indicate such an entity, expresses being and not the *what*, as it happens instead when we say bread, house, tree" (M. Heidegger, *Essere e tempo*, Longanesi, Milano 1976, p. 64).

The only sure characteristic of human essence is its own existence. Therefore, from this assumption, man is what he decides to be; he is free. Even the term existential can be easily misunderstood. Usually by existent we mean what is purely present or given, but what more properly characterizes human reality is that it is not a given; man is openness to all that he can be; he is, precisely, free to choose what he wants to become. As Aristotle had already intuited, persistently behaving in a given way determines, in fact, the character that follows. That is why our being, our essence, is something we do, not something we find. It is only by channeling the abilities and characteristics of our person into a precise configuration among the possibilities of life that we can become a particular individual, realizing ourselves in a given direction.[18] To state that "existence precedes essence" means to recognize that man is at first simply existing, making his appearance on the scene with his own incipient possibilities and missed aspirations, and then activating himself in reworking his own qualities, constitutive of his essence, within the framework of a definitive life plan. In the first stage he is still an incomplete, decompressed figure in potency, ready, however, to redeem himself to realize his full potential. This difference between man and other entities is explained by Sartre with the example of the letter opener (or any other manufactured object).

> This object was constructed by an artisan, having, even before actually producing it, the idea of its function, its concept, thus the essence of the letter opener precedes existence; one could not create such an object if one did not already have its concept in mind. The opposite happens in man. [...] If God does not exist, there is at least one being in whom existence precedes essence, a being that exists before it can be defined by any concept: this being is man, or, as Heidegger says, human reality. What does it mean in this case that existence precedes essence? It means that man exists initially, is found, arises in the world, and is defined afterwards. Man, according to the existentialist conception, is not definable in that at the beginning he is nothing. He will be only later, and he will be what he has made himself. Thus, there is no human nature, since there is no God to conceive it. Man

---

[18] "But what is this self? [...] it is the most abstract thing of all, which at the same time in itself is the most concrete - it is freedom. [...] He who chooses himself discovers that that self which he chooses has an infinite multiplicity in itself. It has a history; a history in which he recognizes his identity with himself" (S. Kierkegaard, *Aut-aut*, op. cit., pp. 72–74).

is not just what one conceives, but what one wants, and precisely what one conceives after existence and wants after this impetus toward existence: Man is nothing but what he makes himself. This is the first principle of existentialism.[19]

Man exists, he is thrown into the world, free to choose what he wants to become. The absence of God lies at the heart of Sartre's moral philosophy: "If God does not exist, then all is permitted,"[20] there can be no a priori justification of any kind of morality. Sartre's ethics assigns all freedom and responsibility for choice to man. For existentialists, life is mission and challenge. Man is given the option of choosing whether to retreat before his responsibilities, pretending that his behavior is dictated by force majeure, and circumstances beyond his will, or to embrace the freedom of being solely responsible for creating a life lived with lucidity, integrity, and courage. The idea of being solely responsible for the course, and the development of one's existence, is immortalized in Pindar's ancient maxim, later picked up by Nietzsche and Heidegger, before being acquired by Jung's analytical psychology, for which man must become what he is.[21]

[19] J.-P. Sartre, *L'esistenzialismo è un umanismo*, op. cit., pp. 25–29.
[20] Ibid., p. 40.
[21] Pindaro, *Pitiche*, II, 72, where it reads "γένοι᾽, οἷος ἐσσὶ μαθών" (become what you are, having learned it).

CHAPTER 6

Transcendence and Freedom

Abstract The chapter investigates the ineluctability of choice in its existential connotation. Freedom is such an inalienable component of man that it does not merely affect his actions or behavior, but it shapes his very thoughts and perception of reality. Freedom and responsibility are therefore unavoidable aspects of human existence, or to put it in Sartre's words man is "condemned to be free."

Keywords Amiel • Choice • Responsibility • Freedom • Sartre • Kant • Husserl

Our being trapped in a world with specific attributes and predefined social relations is part of our giveness as human beings. We are always thrown into a specific context and faced with certain values established by the customs of a given community in history. It has been seen, however, how this giveness is only one dimension of human existence, since humans have, unlike other animals, the capacity to transcend their immediate nature. Because we are passionate and reflective beings, each of us has chosen to define ourselves as a specific configuration of meanings among the many possible in the world. As beings who transcend their embodiment, each of us is able to form our own identity through our actions. To be a man, therefore, means to surpass the shadow of our determination and then to modify and interpret it in the light of a long-term plan of

R. Pugliese, *The Dizziness of Freedom in Kierkegaard and Sartre*, https://doi.org/10.1007/978-3-031-38138-6_6

existence. In his *Journal* (1883–1884), Henri-Frédéric Amiel provides some interesting insights about overcoming the self, in a more eminently literary context:

> I like to dive into the ocean of life, but I do not always succeed without losing my sense of axis and north, without losing myself and feeling the consciousness of my vocation waver. [...] In voluntary surrender to generality, universality, infinity, my specificness evaporates, like a drop of water in a furnace; and it only recondenses when the cold returns, the enthusiasm is extinguished, and the sense of reality has returned. Expansion and condensation, abandonment and recovery of self, conquest of the world and deepening of consciousness: such is the play of the interior life, the journey of the microcosmic spirit, the song of the individual soul with the universal soul, the fruitful grasp of the finite with the infinite.[1]

This is the dimension of transcendence that existentialists speak of. Importantly, the process of re-evaluating and re-interpreting a life occurs often unconsciously as we are busily going about our daily routine. Often the kind of life we choose is the commonly accepted and socially respected one. But even though this process may take place unconsciously, this does not detract from the fact that we are still determining our life and identity in the course of our actions. Whatever we do—or do not do—there will always be an interpenetration between our acting and our being; we are what we do, but we also do what we are. Even detachment, nihilism, and apathy are always potential attitudes to choose from. We are taking on this given identity, even if we believe we are doing nothing. Even the refusal to make a choice is, itself, a choice. Choosing not to choose is still choosing. Thus, it could be argued that even for Nietzsche, nihilism—the death of God, the fall of all values, the dismantling of morality—is nevertheless a *habitus*. Since we are the totality of our actions, the totality of what we do (or fail to do) in the course of life, there is no way to avoid the fact that we are continually choosing ourselves as particular people through our works and omissions.

This idea of individual choice as a determinant in the development of personhood represents the core of existentialist theories of freedom. To say that man is capable of transcending his own giveness is to affirm that he is always faced with a range of possible life paths for the future. For existentialist philosophers, nothing forces us to choose one specific path

---

[1] H.F. Amiel, *Frammenti di un giornale intimo*, UTET, Torino 1967, pp. 77–78.

over another. If we go on with our usual activities in everyday life, it is only because we want to, because we have chosen to, to the extent that our choice is renewed daily. Such is the identity we assume for ourselves. As Sartre would say, we are "condemned to be free," we are free in the sense that for each of the choices we have made, we could have acted differently and that we are always and completely responsible for our actions. Freedom is an inescapable component of human existence. Whether we recognize it or not, we are solely responsible for the kind of people we come to be.

Moreover, freedom is not limited to our ability to choose and direct the course of life, if it is true that for existentialists everyone is also responsible for the way the world around him appears to him. To better grasp this concept, it is appropriate to make a brief reference to Kant. In the *Critique of Pure Reason* (1781), Kant argues that the world we encounter in everyday life is quite different from what the world actually is, a world independent of the way we think and act. Kant argues precisely that the familiar world we encounter is constituted and defined through the set of our categories of thought and perception. We encounter and interact with objects having a precise spatial-temporal location and arranged according to laws of causality not because time, space, and causality are actual constituents of reality as such, but because our minds generate a grid of thought that causes what surrounds us to reveal itself to us as a plurality of spatial-temporal objects arranged in causal relations. So the world we experience on a daily basis is merely the projection of our way of thinking and perceiving reality. For Kant, the world around us is coherent and knowable exclusively as a product of the human capacity to articulate and conceptualize it.[2]

Kant looks at his own thinking as a new Copernican revolution. Copernicus is credited with a series of astronomical observations related to the discovery of the heliocentric system. Similarly, Kant was able to shed light on many aspects of modern thought by asserting that the reality that everyone experiences is formed by the human mind. As noted above, the existentialists take up Kant in the concept that reality (the noumenon) is not knowable in itself but will always and inevitably be filtered and modulated according to human experience, and that the world before our eyes is nothing but will and representation. Despite this initial debt to Kantian thought, the existentialists differ from the Königsberg philosopher in some respects. First of all, Kant regards this process of human mediation

---

[2] C. Guignon, D. Pereboom, *Existentialism*, op. cit. p. XXVII.

as an automatically occurring event that is always the same for all men without distinction, whereas for the existentialists it is our free and individual choice, unique and unrepeatable because it is different for each person, which determines the appearance of a world. Second, Kant believes that it is mental activity—the work of a "transcendental ego"—that transforms our immediate perceptions into a set of ordered experiences, whereas existentialists are convinced that it is actions, relations, and behaviors applied to concrete contexts that define the world as we know it.

The influence of the Kantian perspective is also especially evident in Kierkegaard and Nietzsche. Although both of them reject the Kantian assumption that there are universal and immutable thought structures inherent in human nature, each nevertheless seems to pick up on its legacy by suggesting that reality manifests itself to each according to his or her own point of view. For Kierkegaard, who insisted on the immeasurable value and infinite potential latent in each individual, truth is essentially subjectivity.[3] The world therefore takes on a particular configuration depending on the eye that looks at it, shaped by the sphere of existence in which the individual comes to be. Nietzsche also argues that reality is in fact knowable and accessible only through a particular perspective; in a world now stripped of absolute truths and deprived of any metaphysical certainty, the only truth to which man can aspire is the relative truth of interpretation. Similar to the perception of colors, which cannot be established with absolute certainty for each of us, Nietzsche's thought appeals to the realization that there is no pure, unconditional access to things, but only the deceptive factiousness, the limited perspective of a gaze. Amiel seems to intervene in support of such a conception:

> The center of life is neither in thought, nor in feeling, nor in the will, nor even in consciousness as it thinks, feels or wills, for a moral truth may have been penetrated or possessed in all these ways and still elude us. Deeper than consciousness is being, our very substance, our nature. Only those truths that have entered the latter region, become ourselves, become spontaneous and involuntary, instinctive and unconscious, are really our life, that is, more than our property. As long as we distinguish any space between truth and us,

---

[3] See "All that is essentially real exists for me only insofar as I myself surely exist. Nor do we limit ourselves to being; our existence is entrusted to us as a seat and as a bodily form for the realization of our original individuality" (K. Jaspers, *La filosofia dell'esistenza*, op. cit., p. 16).

we are outside of it. Thought, feeling, desire, and consciousness of life are not yet completely life.[4]

In addition to Kantian experience, it would nevertheless be wrong to misrecognize the influence of Edmund Husserl's phenomenology on existentialist thought. Husserl emphasizes the fact that human experience has as its characteristic feature that it is directed toward objects (what is defined by the term *intentionality*). Every act of consciousness is indeed intentional, that is, it is a tending to something as its specific object. But for Husserl, as for Kant before him, our relating to external entities never means simple and direct absorption of what they are in themselves, independent of our perspective. Rather, ours is an experience always mediated by the human intent to confer meaning and significance on things. Man's capability to record a given event depends entirely on the meaning he decides to attribute to his experience. The contribution of Husserl's thought is paramount in showing that the world we experience is always a product of our interpretation and of our attributing meaning to it. For Husserl, we ourselves are the source of the world we experience; it is but a reflection of our perception and will.

Following in the footsteps of Husserl, existentialists reveal to us how the role that a person chooses to assume in life will govern in advance his or her perspective of existence; in other words, the way the world will appear to that given person is directly dependent on one's point of view. Heidegger describes the world we encounter in everyday life as very different from the one conceived in detached, objective theoretical reflection. And the pages Sartre dedicates to this topic present vivid descriptions of how everything in the world is colored and invested with the meaning that a particular individual wants to attribute to it. For existentialists there is a mutual interplay between facts, the situations in which we come to find ourselves, and our interpretations as agents of them. The factual circumstances of our lives depend on our acting in certain contexts. Moreover, since there are many ways in which an individual can respond and react to a given situation, the same situation can take on innumerable meanings for him.

What all this means for Husserl is to say that each of us is fully responsible through our actions for how the world appears to him. Husserl writes:

[4] H.F. Amiel, *Frammenti di un giornale intimo*, op. cit., pp. 83–84.

I may owe much, perhaps almost everything, to others, but even they are, first of all, others for me who receive from me whatever meaning or validity they may have for me. They can be of assistance to me as fellow subjects only after they have received their meaning and validity from me. As transcendental ego I am thus the absolutely responsible subject of whatever has existential validity for me.[5]

With these words, Husserl seems to suggest that we are all connected to one another through an infinite series of interdependent relationships, and that everything else around the self (people and things) is expressed and thought of as a function of the value and meaning that the self will want to give it. Sartre says something similar when he states that although there are factors in the environment around us that seem to constrain our interpretive activity, they should ultimately be considered simply as opportunities, in the sense that it is up to us to determine what weight they will have for us. For Sartre, as for Kant and Husserl, facts and events are never accessible to man per se, but only in terms of how he decides to interpret them. This means that the individual deliberately chooses the meaning of all reality, including that of the social framework he has created for his own interpretation. In Sartre's words

Giveness is everywhere, but it is inappreciable: I encounter nothing but my own responsibility. … Since others are but chances and opportunities [for my interpretative activity], the responsibility of the it-selfness [i.e., of my interpreting] extends to the whole world as to a world of people.[6]

It is this awareness of our responsibility to the world that is manifested in the experience of "anguish." "It is precisely in this way that conscience discovers itself in anguish: anguished insofar as it exists, since it is obligated to decide what being means within oneself and everywhere outside."[7] Existentialist philosophers tend to believe that it is possible to experience reality only through interpretation, and consequently the real is accessible in ever new and different ways and forms.

---

[5] E. Husserl, *Phenomenology and Anthropology*, trans. R.G. Schmitt, in R.M. Chisholm (ed.), Realism and the Background of Phenomenology, The Free Press, Glencoe (ILL) 1960, p. 138.
[6] J.-P. Sartre, *L'essere e il nulla*, Il Saggiatore, Milano 2014, p. 631.
[7] Ibid. p. 632

CHAPTER 7

Authenticity and Responsibility

Abstract The chapter discusses the concept of authenticity as introduced by existentialist philosophers. Following the maxim of the Oracle of Delphi, "Know thyself," a person must break away from the encrusting of societal norms and expectations to find their true value. Thrown and abandoned into an absurd and meaningless world, man must overcome alienation and external pressures and become congruent with his true self through responsibility.

Keywords Society • Authenticity • Responsibility • Anxiety • Sartre • Nietzsche • Heidegger

For existentialists, in everyday life we tend to allow ourselves to be passively drawn into communal behavior, absorbed by the dictatorship of *one* ("*one* says," "*one* does"). Such is the mechanism whereby the social identity of the self, its deep truth, is not determined and recognized in itself, but occurs through others. Not being sufficient to itself, the self needs others in order to receive recognition. This loss of determination of identity is healed only through others' justification of our reason for being. This creates alienation and detachment from oneself; this is the existential misunderstanding that leads one to trust others' judgment more than one's own. This psychological fracture is perfectly captured by Sartre in the postulate "hell is other people." Freedom, which for Sartre coincides

R. Pugliese, *The Dizziness of Freedom in Kierkegaard and Sartre*, https://doi.org/10.1007/978-3-031-38138-6_7

with the very structure of existence, throws the individual into a state of endemic and permanent conflict with others.

> Everything that applies to me, applies to others. As I try to free myself from the influence of others, the other tries to free himself from mine; as I try to subjugate the other, the other tries to subjugate me. [...] Conflict is the original state of being-for-others.[1]

In Sartre's universe, the clash of liberty and the war of meanings are ontologically unavoidable; the conflict with others, more or less veiled, is consequently a structural characteristic of the human condition. The common morality dictates to us what should be said and done, dictating to us norms and conventions and conducting our behavior. Following the silent tyranny of conformity, we comply by thus doing what must be done, believing that our lives are justified in their highest purpose as long as we adapt to the commonly accepted customs and habits of our social reality. We are all "conformist censors,"[2] quick to flatten ourselves into the crowd and to correct others. There is, at least in the modern world, an exaggerated pressure toward what Michel Foucault called "normalization"[3]: the standardization of every aspect of life with the intent of creating and sustaining a regimented and controlled set of predefined social practices.

The specter of conformity and its implications on the uniqueness of the individual have been considered by more than one author. Kierkegaard speaks of the public and its leveling all differences between individuals. The moment everything exceptional is reduced to commonplace, and any substantial difference is erased, it becomes extremely difficult to find something in the present that has true meaning, an absolute value in our existence. When nothing genuinely stands out for its validity, then life turns into a desolate succession of episodes without coherence or direction. Life proceeds "as confusedly as the writing of ancient manuscripts, without any punctuation, one word, one sentence after another."[4] In order to become authentic, the individual must stand up against the wall of mass and of *one*, exalting himself in his own singularity to finally arrive at being one and himself.

---

[1] J.-P. Sartre, *L'essere e il nulla*, op. cit. p. 424.
[2] J. Haugeland, Heidegger on Being a Person, "Nous," 16 (1982), pp. 6–26.
[3] C. Guignon, D. Pereboom, *Existentialism*, op. cit. p. XXXI.
[4] S. Kierkegaard, *Il concetto dell'angoscia*, op. cit. p. 94.

One of the most ruthless critiques of contemporary conduct of life and communal morality is found in Nietzsche's description of the herd in the *Genealogy of Morals* (1887). For Nietzsche, the purported transcendent values of morality are merely a projection of certain human tendencies. Even the so-called voice of conscience, the basis of morality itself, is nothing more than the presence in us of the social authorities by which we have been educated. In the *Posthumous Fragments* (1887) Nietzsche points out that instead of being "the voice of God in the breast of man," conscience is rather "the voice of some men in man." Morality for Nietzsche is nothing more than the herd instinct in the individual, that is, his subjection to certain directives set by the exponents of the ruling elites. Metaphysics, morality, reason, and science would be nothing more than survival lies, consolatory perspectives contrived for the sole purpose of believing in life. Considered from a psychological and historical perspective, ethical values do not therefore represent autonomous ontological entities but are "the result of certain utility perspectives for the maintenance and reinforcement of forms of human domination; and only falsely are they projected into the essence of things."

> That there is no truth; that there is no absolute constitution of things, a "thing in itself"; this itself is a nihilism, is indeed extreme nihilism. It places the value of things precisely in the fact that this value does not correspond nor has corresponded to any reality, but only a symptom of force on the part of those who place value, a simplification for the purposes of life.[5]

According to Nietzsche, our existence as social animals tends to domesticate us. It obscures all that is creative and unique in us, prompting us to view ourselves through standardized and socially approved categories. We become docile and well-behaved conformists, unable to be original. Although Nietzsche is highly critical of herd life, he does not reject the idea of community in its entirety. He, for example, praises on several occasions the "noble morality" of the ancient Greeks, regarded as a superior model of civilization compared to the degenerate individualism of modernity.

The works of Heidegger and Sartre carry forward the existentialist critique of communal life. Sartre makes fun of the bourgeoisie's pompous "spirit of seriousness" and firmly stigmatizes the process that drags the

---

[5] F. Nietzsche, *Frammenti postumi*, Opere complete, II, Adelphi, Milano 1971, p. 14.

individual within an us. "He who feels himself as constituting an us with other men feels swallowed up by an infinity of foreign existences, is alienated radically and without appeal."[6] Like Nietzsche, Sartre nevertheless aims, in *Existentialism is a Humanism*, at an image of an ideal society, an idea that echoes the Kantian notion of a federation of peoples, a cosmopolitan ordering among peoples, characterized by reciprocity and recognition among all its members. Finally, Heidegger attacks the drowsiness of consciousness and alienation from self that is typical of the way we conform to society. As ordinary beings, we tend to become interchangeable pieces of the same common mosaic, acting out our parts in various social dramas, all constantly guided by socially accepted norms and conventions. The roles and parts we come to play are anonymous in the sense that anyone could take our place and replace us. For most of our existence therefore, we are simply anonymous sets of roles and routines that any other person with the same qualities as us could adopt. Heidegger writes:

> In the use of means of transportation, in the means of transmission of information, each is like the other. Such a being-together completely dissolves the individual being-ness in the way of being of others, so that others are increasingly diluted in their diversity and concreteness. In this irrelevance and impersonality the *one* exercises its authentic dictatorship.[7]

In our mundane activities, all we do is to do what *one* is supposed to do, following the procedures drawn up by communal life. Even in their rebellion against the rules and customs of society, people tend to embrace and express themselves in accordance with specific social norms. For Heidegger, we exist as *one* (but the German expression *das Man* takes on even more of a gnomic, universal meaning).

We take pleasure and enjoy ourselves as *one* [*man*] takes pleasure; we read, see and judge about literature and art as *one* sees and judges; likewise we shrink back from the 'masses of people' as *one* shrinks back; we find 'shocking' what *one* finds 'shocking'.[8]

The *one*, which is not any determined being, but all, determines the way of being in everyday life. For Heidegger, however, and here is the

---

[6] J.-P. Sartre, *L'essere e il nulla*, op. cit. p. 482.

[7] M. Heidegger, *Essere e Tempo*, Halle, 1927, pp. 126–127.

[8] Idem., *Being and Time*, cited in C. Guignon, D. Pereboom, Existentialism, op. cit. p. XXXIII.

turning point, such a condition (man's presenting himself as *one*) is but a "primordial phenomenon" and can therefore be overcome. Kierkegaard, Heidegger, Sartre; for all these philosophers man is able to free himself from his complacent and anonymous sinking into society. But redemption will not come through lucid reflection or rational mediation, rather with a radical life change that originates from a deep emotional experience. Kierkegaard speaks of the despair that accompanies man's becoming lost in an ordinary and impersonal existence, the process that leads him to experience the death of the ego, that is, the denial of the human attempt to make himself self-sufficient and to escape from self. The despair Kierkegaard describes is not the "finite" despair that descends from the loss of worldly goods—such as the loss of a loved one or an inheritance—but the infinite despair that descends in man from the awareness of his own existential insufficiency. Yet it is precisely such an experience that proves to be salvific for man; for only after he has touched bottom will he be able to rise to the surface. The individual must therefore embrace despair, wanting it with all of himself, for it is only by recognizing himself in the grip of it that he can finally turn in search of salvation. Heidegger, implicitly recognizing Kierkegaard's profound influence on his own thought, similarly speaks to us of anguish as the state of mind in which man discovers himself abandoned to himself and consequently the only one responsible for attributing meaning to his life. Finally, Sartre speaks of nausea as the feeling through which being reveals itself to itself for what it is, and of anguish and the sense of abandonment that guide man to recognize that he alone is responsible for defining and interpreting the world around him. For all these thinkers, man's awakening from his condition as a passive spectator in the theater of the world takes place as a traumatic process, as a painful unveiling of a part of himself and as an unconscious "unrolling of the mysterious scroll of the self," rather than an explicit and cognitive awareness.

What such an intense emotional experience reveals is the possibility of a transformed way of being, of a self in transit on the tracks of becoming and freedom. Those who have survived the grip of nothingness, of uniformity and apathy, find a world wide open at their feet as a playground of the divine. In *The Gay Science* (1882) Nietzsche describes with euphoria the joyous scenario that awaits all those who have left behind the death of God and the initial nihilistic disenchantment; the possibility of playing naively but seriously, like children, "with everything to which the name of sacred was hitherto given, good, untouchable, divine." Heidegger, in a quite different register, speaks of the "sober joy" of authentic existence, in which the individual, having become aware of his own being-for-death, decisively appropriates the possibilities that history (his own history as a man) offers him. Although Sartre's definition of authentic existence in *Being and Nothingness* is ambiguous to say the least, he undoubtedly believes that it is possible to acquire one's freedom with transparency, lucidity, intensity, and a commitment that takes the form of a fundamental life plan. For Kierkegaard, the highest goal of human existence consists of the self becoming one with the power that constitutes it.

This then is the formula that describes the condition of the self when despair is completely eradicated: by relating itself to its own self, and by willing to be itself, the self is grounded transparently in the Power that constituted it.[9]

The concept of authenticity should call us back from our state of distraction and dispersion in the world. By shaking us out of our torpor, it urges us to live intensely and with focus, a new way of being that integrates beliefs, feelings, and desires into an organic *unicum*. The founding characteristic of an authentic life is to focus on a fundamental plan that gives value, coherence, and integrity to our lives; a supreme purpose around which to organize our otherwise ordinary existence.

The thinkers mentioned so far have offered their essential contributions to what Foucault calls the "art of existing" in the modern age. The mere fact that the ideas of Kierkegaard, Nietzsche, Heidegger, and Sartre still appear so "risky," sometimes inconvenient, strikingly topical, and difficult to implement, should help us understand their modernity and the permanence of their value. Each of these authors invites us, as individuals, to not adhere uncritically to a particular school of thought, challenging us to think about things autonomously, inwardly, and silently, and to arrive at a final decision using our critical consciousness. This emphasis on the responsibility of the individual to manage and give meaning and content to his or her existence is probably existentialism's most important contribution to philosophy.

---

[9] Kierkegaard, *The Sickness unto Death*, quoted in C. Guignon, D. Pereboom, *Existentialism*, op. cit. p. XXXIV.

CHAPTER 8

Freedom as Destiny

Abstract The last chapter focuses on existential freedom in what has been its most radical formulation by Jean-Paul Sartre. According to Sartre, existence must constantly supersede essence since a person is more than their immediate characteristics and has no choice but to exercise freedom through responsibility. Man is therefore "condemned to be free," and the will to shape his life becomes an inalienable component of personality.

Keywords Agency • Freedom • Responsibility • Choice • Sartre • Essence • Existence

Of the thinkers who have appeared so far, Sartre is the only one who has explicitly called himself an existentialist.[1] And it was Sartre who coined the expression "existence precedes essence," which has now become one of the most celebrated formulations of existentialism. To say that existence precedes essence is to say that what man is, the meaning of his life, is not something predetermined and immutable, and that although there is in him an innate component of certain characteristics by virtue of which he comes to be, man himself will later be able to exist differently by becoming responsible for himself through freedom. In other words, in man, essence

---

[1] E. Kern, *Sartre: A Collection of Critical Essays*, op. cit. pp. 2–3.

is not something given once and for all, as it might be for the letter opener, for example, rather it is the inescapable basis for building one's existence made up of choices, renunciations, failures, successes, risks, and plans. Aristotle defined the essence of a thing as the sum of the characteristics that make that thing precisely what it is and not another, and without which it would cease to be what it is. In the case of man, the basic requirement was to be in the presence of an organism with a particular biological structure and endowed with a certain intellectual potential without which that given entity could not be said to be human.

For Sartre there are in fact entities in which essence precedes existence. For example, work tools. In the case of the hammer, its essence—the fact that it was created for a particular purpose, that is, hammering nails into the wall—perfectly coincides with its existence by defining the nature of the tool-hammer through its specific function. In the hammer, "existence precedes existence" means that a particular object, in order to exist as a hammer, must have the ability to drive nails into the wall as a foundational characteristic.

For man, on the contrary, it is existence that precedes essence. First of all, because there are no fixed and determined characteristics for existing as human beings. Sartre's perspective is in sharp contrast to the religious belief of a God who creates humans and their essence, endowing them with determinate characteristics that form their intrinsic nature. For Sartre this essentialism is unacceptable once the individual becomes aware of the power of the Nietzschean announcement of the death of God. In the absence of any otherworldly absolute and of any metaphysical superstructure, as well as of a first principle governing the universe, the classical idea of a predetermined set of values and characteristics establishing man's true nature and his specific function on earth also fails.

> And when it comes to abandonment [...] we just mean that God does not exist and that one must draw the consequences of this fact to the end. Existentialism vigorously opposes a certain kind of secular morality that would like to get God out of the way at the least expense.[2] [...] Existentialism on the contrary thinks that it is very inconvenient that God does not exist, since with God vanishes all possibility of finding values in an intelligible

---

[2] Sartre wants here to firmly oppose a certain secular morality constituted in France beginning in the 1880s that dismissed God as a difficult and "costly" tenet, instead proposing a set of values (honesty, progress, humanism) to be taken seriously and regarded as existing a priori.

heaven; there can no longer be an a priori good since there is no infinite and perfect consciousness to think it; nowhere is it written that good exists, that one must be honest, that one must not lie, and for this precise reason: we are in a place where there is only man. Dostoevsky wrote, "If God does not exist everything is allowed." Here is the starting point of existentialism. Everything is actually permissible if God does not exist, and consequently man is "abandoned" because he does not find, either in himself or outside himself, possibilities to anchor himself. And first of all, he does not find excuses. If indeed existence precedes essence, explanations can never be given referring to a given and fixed human nature; in other words, there is no determinism: man is free, man is freedom.[3]

As mentioned earlier, to affirm that "existence precedes essence" is to recognize that man is at first simply existing, making his appearance on the scene among other beings, without any particular attributes and lacking a plan that determines who he is and what he should do. Therefore, there is neither a specific human configuration nor a proper function, genetic code, or neuro-physiology that fixes an individual's identity in a predetermined set of traits and purposes.[4] Sartre expresses this idea dramatically by writing that human beings find themselves abandoned in a world they have not chosen, adrift among other beings without a precise identity that gives meaning to their lives. After this initial phase of existential bewilderment, however, each of us is able to re-invent ourselves and our own essence through our own actions, and, especially, through what Sartre calls *projet*, that is, with a life plan we freely choose. On the other hand, there is no single essence for all humanity; rather each of us will be able to create our own through a plan to be chosen and evaluated. This redemption of the individual involves each person's choosing his or her own identity and characteristics through the realization of a plan. Man then is nothing but what he makes himself, a being capable of self-determination in the course of his life.

In *Existentialism is a Humanism* Sartre says of man that "in the beginning he is nothing, [...] he will be only later, and he will be what he has made himself."[5] Since we arise in the world without certain characteristics that distinguish us as a specific being from another, from the beginning we merely exist as a mere nothingness. The threat of nothingness as the

---

[3] J.-P. Sartre, *L'esistenzialismo è un umanismo*, op. cit., pp. 38–41.
[4] C. Guignon, D. Pereboom, *Existentialism*, op. cit. p. 257.
[5] J.-P. Sartre, *L'esistenzialismo è un umanismo*, op. cit., p. 28.

nullifying power of what is possible, as the annihilating power of any alternative of existence probably constitutes Sartre's most obvious debt to Heidegger and, consequently, to Kierkegaard himself. Like Heidegger, Sartre in *Being and Nothingness* questions the structures of being. Sartre proceeds phenomenologically, dividing being between in-itself (the given) and for-itself (consciousness). The first type of being represents everything that is not consciousness but with which consciousness enters into relation. The for-itself, on the other hand, is identified with consciousness itself, which has the prerogative of attributing meanings to things in the world. Sartre calls the for-itself "nothingness," understood not as the opposite of being but as consciousness itself, that is, the nullifying power of the pure given and as the source of meanings with respect to the in-itself. To say that man is consciousness or for-itself is thus equivalent to saying that man is free, since it denies reality in the light of meanings that govern it. For Sartre, freedom is the permanent possibility of the rupture or nullification of consciousness of the world that constitutes the very structure of existence.[6]

> I am condemned to always live beyond my essence, beyond the motives and reasons for my act; I am condemned to be free. This would mean that no other boundaries beyond itself would be found to my freedom or, if you will, it would mean that we are not free to be free.[7]

For Sartre, freedom is inseparable from the reality of the human condition and must be sought beyond free will and specific volitions, being rooted in the innermost structure of existence. It follows that it is not liberty that is an expression of will, but vice versa.[8]

> An existence that, as consciousness, is necessarily separate from all others, because they are not related to it except insofar as they are for it, that decides on its past in the form of tradition in the light of its future, instead of letting it purely and simply determine its present, and that lets something else

---

[6] C.O. Schrag, *Existence and Freedom: Towards an Ontology of Human Finitude*, Northwestern University Press, Evanston, Illinois 1961, p. 42; E. Kern, *Sartre: A Collection of Critical Essays*, op. cit. p. 9.

[7] J.-P. Sartre, *L'essere e il nulla*, op. cit. p. 506.

[8] C.O. Schrag, *Existence and Freedom*, op. cit. pp. 177–179.

announce what it is, by itself, meaning by an end that it is not and that it projects beyond the world, here is what we call a free existence.[9]

Freedom is not so much about individual acts and decisions as it is about the fundamental plan in which they are included and which constitutes the ultimate possibility of human reality, its original choice. The fundamental plan certainly leaves room for volition and desires, but the original freedom is inherent in the choice of the plan itself. And it is an unconditional freedom, destined by ontological constitution to be free. Sartre thus moves from a deterministic-deliberative context (where every decision is made based on the valuation of external objective reasons) to an ontological and psychic one where man is responsible even for his own passions. In what reads like a Kierkegaardian passage, Sartre tells us that "the anguish which, after being unveiled, reveals our freedom to our consciousness is a testament to this continuous modification of our initial plan."[10] Man is constantly threatened by the nullification inherent in his choice, constantly threatened with choosing himself, and thus becoming different from what he is. The necessity of constantly having to choose oneself that is imposed on man since he is nothing is the sword of Damocles of our condition, which condemns us to be free. Such considerations introduce what for Sartre is a fundamental category: human responsibility.

> If existence truly precedes essence, man is responsible for what he is. Thus, the first step of existentialism is put every man in possession of who he is and to bring down upon him the total responsibility for his own existence. And, when we say that man is responsible for himself, we do not mean that man is responsible for his own contained individuality, but that he is responsible for all men. [...] The man who makes a commitment and is aware that he is not only the one who chooses to be, but also a lawgiver who chooses, at the same time, and for himself and for all mankind, cannot escape the feeling of his own complete and profound responsibility.[11]

It becomes evident how, for Sartre, everything that happens in the world goes back to the liberty and responsibility of original choice; nothing that happens to man can in fact be called inhuman.

---

[9] J.-P. Sartre, *L'essere e il nulla*, op. cit. p. 521.
[10] Ibid. p. 533.
[11] J.-P. Sartre, *L'esistenzialismo è un umanismo*, op. cit., pp. 30 and 33–34.

Everything that happens to me is mine. [...] The most heinous situations of war, the worst tortures do not create inhuman states of affairs: there are no inhuman situations; it is only out of fear, flight and recourse to magic behavior that I will decide on the inhuman; but this decision is human and I will bear all the responsibility for it.[12]

It is man who decides the adversity coefficient of events and even their unpredictability to the extent that he decides about himself. Consequently, there are no accidental instances, or sudden social events that drag man from the brink. If the individual is called to war, this war is his war, it is in his own image, and he deserves it:

I deserve it first because I could always evade it by suicide or desertion: these extreme possibilities must always be present when considering a situation. Since I did not evade it, I chose it: this may be out of weakness, out of cowardice in the face of public opinion, because I prefer certain values to that of the refusal of waging war. [...] In any case it is a choice.[13]

The unavoidable appeal to human responsibility and its crushing weight is taken by Sartre to new extremes and sounds distressing and disorienting in an age that has learned to make de-responsibilization its trench. Exemption from obligations and duties, hypocrisy toward oneself and others, apathy, extreme individualism, and de-responsibilization seem the only weapons left to man in a distant and cruel world. Against this attitude Sartre stoically reminds us that there is also another way of living; his is the inevitable reminder of the responsibility the individual cannot escape and the infinite power of *no*. Of course, it is not easy to translate Sartre's teaching into reality; states of mind such as anguish, nausea, solitude, and despair become the indispensable passport for those who venture beyond the frontier of freedom in search of their true self. The path of the self is constantly exposed to risk and existential shipwreck that drags the being

---

[12] Idem., *Essere e nulla*, op. cit. p. 629. For further insight on the concept of freedom taken to its extreme consequences see the essay by K. Jaspers, *La questione della colpa. Sulla responsabilità politica della Germania*, Cortina Raffaello, Milano 1996.

[13] J.-P. Sartre, *Essere e nulla*, op. cit. p. 629.

adrift, and yet freedom is worth this risk; indeed freedom is itself the risk.[14] For Jaspers, too, knowledge can never get to explain the world, as a multiple, dynamic, elusive reality that escapes its capacity for synthesis. Transcendence eludes the reach of thought. Jaspers' concept of shipwreck is the rare condition through which existence can sense transcendence, through experiencing limit situations.

> Finally, there is the shipwreck. [...] The shipwreck awaits the end of all that is generally called to the presence of thought; what was valid in the horizon of the relative, embedded in the logical world, shipwrecks. [...] The world, in fact, is not an absolute and in itself concluded being that allows itself to be scrutinized down to its ultimate foundation, nor on the other hand is the cognitive process able to completely traverse an organic reality. [...] In borderline situations it becomes manifest that everything that is positive for us is linked to the negative, which, while opposing it, belongs to it. There is no good that is not also an evil possibility and reality, there is no truth without falsehood, no life without death; all happiness is conjoined with sorrow, all achievement with risk and loss. The depth of the human soul, in which Transcendence makes its word heard, is connected in fact to disorder, pathology, extravagance; this connection does not allow itself to be interpreted univocally. [...] When in my freedom, starting from beingness, I come to the consciousness of being, then, precisely in the clearest decision that my personal being takes in order to act, I must experience, in addition to its realization, also its shipwreck.[15]

The meaning of freedom consists for Sartre precisely in the transcendence of the given, in the ability to continuously modify our essence that is not given once and forever. Freedom is not concept, but rebellion, struggle, denial of that instance, and its overcoming. For our life is more than a sum

---

[14] Applying this concept in an anthropological and social context, Margaret Mead identifies unconditional choice as one of the causes of neurosis in Western civilization: "A society that incites choice, in which vociferous groups swarm, each of which wants to impose its own way of salvation, its own special economic policy, will leave no peace to each new generation, until everyone has chosen or succumbs, unable to bear the very conditions of choice" (M. Mead, *Adolescenza in Samoa*, Giunti, Florence 2017, p. 194).

[15] K. Jaspers, *Metafisica*, Mursia, Milan 1972, p. 348.

of circumstances, more than the sum of its individual parts, and we are always more than the whole of our determinations. If we can prove that freedom is the only non-negotiable good, and that its price is eternal vigilance, then perhaps the lesson of centuries of the history of human thought will not have been entirely in vain.

Chronology of Kierkegaard's Life and Major Works

1813   One of seven children, Søren Aabye Kierkegaard is born on May 5 in Copenhagen, to a wealthy family.

1830   Enrolls at the University of Copenhagen to study Theology.

1834   His mother, Ane Sørensdatter Lund Kierkegaard, dies, possibly from typhus.

1837   He meets Regine Olsen for the first time.

1838   His father, Michael Pedersen Kierkegaard, dies at age 82.

1840   He proposes to Regine.

1841   Breaks off engagement to Regine. Attends Schelling's lectures in Berlin, with Mikhail Bakunin, Jacob Burckhardt, and Friedrich Engels. Later that year, he graduates with a *Magister Artium* with a thesis on the concept of irony in reference to Socrates.

1842   Publishes *Either/Or*.

1843   Publishes *Fear and Trembling*.

1844   Publishes *The Concept of Anxiety*.

1846   Exchanges a series of attacks with *The Corsair*, a Danish satirical paper.

1849   Publishes *The Sickness unto Death*.

1854   Embarks on polemic against the Church of Denmark through newspaper articles published in *The Fatherland* and a series of pamphlets called *The Moment*.

1855   Collapses in the street and is taken to the hospital where he will die on November 11.

© The Author(s), under exclusive license to Springer Nature Switzerland AG 2023
R. Pugliese, *The Dizziness of Freedom in Kierkegaard and Sartre*,
https://doi.org/10.1007/978-3-031-38138-6

CHRONOLOGY OF SARTRE'S LIFE AND MAJOR WORKS

1905   Sartre is born in Paris on June 21, the only child of Jean-Baptiste and Anne-Marie.

1906   His father, an officer of the French Navy, dies suddenly.

1917   His mother remarries and the family moves to La Rochelle.

1920   He returns to Paris.

1924   Enrolls in École Normale Supérieur.

1929   He meets Simone de Beauvoir. Finishes first on philosophy *agrégation*, an examination for civil service in secondary and higher education.

1931   Begins teaching at various lycées in the Havre.

1933   Spends year in Berlin at the Institut français d'Allemagne.

1938   He publishes *Nausea*, which received considerable attention.

1939   He publishes *Sketch for a Theory of Emotions*, his first fully fledged philosophical work. At the outbreak of World War II, he is drafted and serves in the French Army as a meteorologist.

1940   He is a war prisoner.

1943   He published *Being and Nothingness*, his major philosophical work.

1944   He helps institute the magazine *Les Temps modernes*.

1945   He publishes the essay *Existentialism is a Humanism*, which contributed to popularize the term and establish Sartre as one of its major representatives.

© The Author(s), under exclusive license to Springer Nature Switzerland AG 2023
R. Pugliese, *The Dizziness of Freedom in Kierkegaard and Sartre*, https://doi.org/10.1007/978-3-031-38138-6

1952   He becomes a Marxist.
1960   He publishes *Critique of Dialectical Reason*, where he tries to rec-
        oncile Marxism with existentialism.
1964   He published his autobiography *Words*. He turns down the Nobel
        Prize in Literature.
1980   He dies in Paris at age 74.

Appendix: Sartre and Cinema

Roberto Pugliese

Can cinema and existentialism coexist? Is cinematic language, as a mode of expression that is by its very nature pre-determined and pre-fixed, compatible with a system of thought that makes individual freedom the core of man's specific and original way of being, even in its relations with society and subsequently with the arts that are expressed in it?

These are complex and thorny questions that Jean-Paul Sartre and Simone de Beauvoir have asked themselves on several occasions (without, however, ever settling on definitive answers), as documented by numerous contributions and writings especially by the former, reported in the most important text dedicated to the rapport between the French philosopher and the seventh art, and to which constant reference will be made here: *Sartre et le cinéma* (Atlantica/Séguier ed., 2005) by Dominique Chateau. Chateau, among the foremost experts on the relations between cinema (and more generally the arts) and philosophy, especially in its ontological ramification, appears, however, mainly interested in finding, in Sartre's thought, the possible traces of a theoretical elaboration in tune with his overall work. He reaches the conclusion that under this aspect—the theoretical one, precisely—cinema interested Sartre very little, while under the aesthetic profile he seemed, on the contrary, to revere it. This helps to explain why, for example, the author of *No Exit* did not seem to particularly appreciate the phenomenon of the Nouvelle Vague (the feeling was mutual: Jean-Luc Godard called Sartre's "the most mediocre of literatures"), detested a seminal work such as Orson Welles' *Citizen Kane*, and

R. Pugliese, *The Dizziness of Freedom in Kierkegaard and Sartre*,
https://doi.org/10.1007/978-3-031-38138-6

instead allowed himself to be seduced by the classic westerns of John Ford or Howard Hawks, completely indifferent to the reactionary and racist ideology that swirled there and of which he was nevertheless perfectly aware.

In other words, it seems to be the exquisitely narrative dimension of cinema that Sartre was most interested in, going so far as to place this form of expression, as Simone de Beauvoir said, almost on the same level as literature: to the detriment, conversely, of theoretical or linguistic elaborations for whose complexity cinematic language seemed decidedly inadequate. Again through de Beauvoir's testimony, we know that Sartre was devoted to silent cinema to the point of doubting that the advent of sound, particularly speech, would supplant its emotional charge: he considered speech incompatible with that sense of "unreality"—comic, poetic, epic—that attracted him to cinema; moreover, he was capable of being moved to tears before Al Jolson singing in *The Jazz Singer* (1927, Alan Crosland) or the spirituals of *Hallelujah!* (1929, King Vidor) or to the Marlene Dietrich of *Der blaue Engel* (1930, Josef von Sternberg). And this is what explains Sartre's fascination with classic Hollywood cinema, stripped of ideologies and any possible instance of "progressivism." One can be a progressive—declared de Beauvoir—and still love John Wayne.

But all this only underscores a widespread contradiction, yesterday as today, in even the most ideologically left-leaning intellectual circles: that is, the one whereby the aesthetic attraction to an object prevails over the awareness of how far away, if not hostile, that object is to us content-wise. This is a debate that has remote origins, and which the decline of ideologies—of which Sartre and de Beauvoir were well aware, despite their limpid but also critical Marxist militancy—has resurfaced, and it is also the reason why, to give just two examples, a film like Leni Riefenstahl's *Triumph des Willens* (1935) appears to us today as a formidable masterpiece of visual architecture and epic cinema, despite the abhorrent Nazi ideology it serves, while Richard Fleischer's *Mandingo* (1975) is with good approximation one of the most horrendous films in the history of cinema, despite the very noble and totally shareable anti-racist intentions.

These considerations seem to identify in Sartre's positions regarding cinema almost an anticipatory attitude to that phenomenon, developed especially since the 1970s, which goes by the definition of cinephilia, and which in turn was a product of the "politique des auteurs" promulgated between the 1950s and 1960s precisely by the exponents of the Nouvelle Vague in the pages of the "Cahiers du Cinéma." All this, however, tells us little about what the philosopher's direct contribution to the seventh art as a writer, screenwriter, and dialogist was. It must be said that Sartre himself did not hold this role in high regard: on the contrary, he considered it essentially a series of failures, some more pronounced than others, probably useful only to ensure some additional income. After all, it is difficult to imagine how the density and plurality of meanings contained in Sartre's texts—and which emerges from his conception of writing—could easily adhere to the needs of simplification, clarity, and communication required by a film script that aims to comply with a narrative structure.

Sartre's filmography is very full-bodied, amounting in all to a hundred titles between his own screenplays, dialogues, stories, adaptations of others, and more or less overt transpositions. This attests to a fairly strong presence of Sartre in cinema, in various guises, and is notable especially in terms of the destination on the big screen of some of his most famous texts.

The greatest point of friction between Sartre and cinema, or rather between Sartre and the Hollywood production machine, occurred in 1962 with the affair concerning *Freud: The Secret Passion*, an ambitious biography of the father of psychoanalysis played by a tormented Montgomery Clift and directed by one of the most embattled exponents of old Hollywood, John Huston. Huston's idea, shared by Universal, of covering his back intellectually by entrusting the screenplay to the philosopher—which, moreover, had always been wary of the psychoanalytic method and inclined to safeguard above all its symbolic aspects—produced as a result a monumental, unrealizable script, which (as Huston had to say) would have required an eight-hour film. The fall-out was inevitable, as was the withdrawal of Sartre's signature from the credits, where two screenwriters from the studio, Charles Kaufman and Wolfgang Reinhardt, took over. They tried to preserve some elements of Sartre's work, especially on the level of the symbols represented and some parts of the dialogue, resulting in a film more interesting for its purely aesthetic aspects (Douglas Slocombe's gloomy black and white photography, Jerry Goldsmith's avant-garde soundtrack) than for its purely cultural significance.

By a strange coincidence, of that same year is *I sequestrati di Altona*, which Vittorio De Sica—one of the fathers of Italian neorealism—drew from the 1959 Sartrian drama *Les sequestrés d'Altona*, but entrusted the screenplay to his faithful collaborator Cesare Zavattini together with Abby Mann, celebrated American screenwriter and playwright, who in 1962 would also win the Oscar for best non-original script with Stanley Kramer's

Judgment at Nuremberg, a work of similar setting, era, and subject matter to De Sica's film. A stellar but unbalanced cast (Fredric March, Sofia Loren, Maximilian Schell), expert artistic contributions (scenes by Renato Guttuso, music based on the Adagio from Dimitri Shostakovich's Symphony No. 11), and a setting of solemn, inescapable tragicness make it an unresolved but fascinating film about the guilt of the vanquished and the damnation of remorse, which are indeed very Sartrian themes.

These are two eccentric titles in the philosopher's filmography, not having seen him involved—especially the former—directly. More obvious traces of his themes are to be found elsewhere in his work as a screenwriter for French cinema, although it would be wrong to expect to find in these scripts the sheer representation of his philosophical system. Still, *Les jeux sont faits* (1947, Jean Delannoy), the first of the scripts written for the Pathé production company, is to this day one of the most "Sartrian" films ever made: in the story of the two lovers who meet in the afterlife and are given a second chance to return to the world of the living, without, however, escaping the fate that awaits them, the fantastic and visionary elaboration of a theme very pertinent to his thought, that of "sursis" or recovery/return, and of the implacable determinism that constitutes an essential element of it is developed. This is, by the way, a narrative core that reaches present day through a great deal of cinema especially on the fantasy and horror side (think of the strand opened in 1993 by Harold Ramis' *Groundhog Day* and continued until *Happy Death Day*, 2017, Christopher Landon, and its sequel), beginning—again in 1947—with that *Repeat performance* by Alfred L. Werker, on a script by Walter Bullock, which appears for all intents and purposes to be a Hollywood remake of Delannoy's film. Redemption, or at least an attempt to access it, is also at the center of *Les Orgueilleux* (1953, Yves Allégret), another screenplay dating from a decade earlier, under the title *Typhus*, but later disowned by Sartre and taken over by the director himself along with Pierre Bost and Jean Aurenche, featuring two stars of French cinema such as Michèle Morgan and especially Gérard Philipe, as a tormented and disenchanted alcoholic doctor grappling with a meningitis epidemic and the onset of an unexpected love affair. All ideological, in contrast, particularly against the McCarthy witch hunt evoked in the historical episode that occurred in Massachusetts in the late seventeenth century, is *Les sorcières de Salem* (1957, Raymond Rouleau), starring the Yves Montand-Simone Signoret couple, which Sartre had made by adapting Arthur Miller's 1953 play *The Crucible*, of the same year. In 1953, the philosopher had also adapted the

1836 play by Alexandre Dumas *Kean, ou désordre et génie*, an adventurous biography of the very popular English actor who lived in the nineteenth century, and that adaptation, filtered through the screenplay by Suso Cecchi D'Amico, Francesco Rosi, and Vittorio Gassman, would flow into the 1956 film, co-signed with Rosi and histrionically played by Gassman himself, *Kean—Genius and Unruliness.*

Strongly political and polemical also appears *La p … respectueuse* (1952, Marcello Pagliero and Charles Brabant), based on the play of the same name from 1946, which Sartre wrote on his return from a trip to the United States and following the dramatic impression left on him by the racial discrimination in the country. Here, Alexandre Astruc (1923–2016), an important figure as a director, screenwriter, critic, and film theorist very close to the philosopher, appears among the authors of the adaptation.

There is no doubt, however, that Sartre's text that has enjoyed the greatest fortune in cinema is the play *Huis-clos*, composed in 1944, at the height of World War II, and first staged at the Théâtre du Vieux-Colombier in Paris on May 27 of that year, only to be published three years later. Indeed, the famous metaphor contained therein in the aphorism "L'enfer sont les autres," claustrophobically embodied in the quartet of characters engaged in detesting each other while in the antechamber of hell, lends itself to very different symbolic representations: in Jacqueline Audry's 1954 version with a script by Pierre Laroche, it is almost a fantasy melodrama; in the titled 1962 Hollywood reinterpretation *No Exit*, directed by Ted Danielewski with (uncredited) input from Orson Welles and with a screenplay by George Tabori, a dark, concentric noir; in Jean-Louis Lorenzi's faithful 2005 TV adaptation a good example of filmed theater; as well as—also for TV—in Edvin Tiemroth's Danish *Lukkede døre* (1959) on a translation by Paul Sarauw, and even more so in 2002 in the gloomy and conflicted reinterpretation by renowned actor and director Robert Hossein.

The next play by Sartre to receive the most film adaptations is *Les mains sales*, from 1948, a controversial and problematic reinterpretation—albeit indirect—of the assassination of Lev Trotsky, former Red Army chief and bitter rival of Stalin, which took place in 1940 in Mexican exile at the hands of a hitman of the Soviet dictator. Conflicts and doubts are raised in the drama that inexorably widen from the individual level to the ideological and political sphere, while rather simplified in the 1951 film version of the same name by Fernand Rivers and Simone Berriau, and instead greatly emphasized in 1978 by the Italian TV miniseries *Le mani sporche*, directed and written by militant director Elio Petri, starring Marcello Mastroianni and Giuliana De Sio. The most original and interesting version, however, is perhaps the one made in 1989, again for television, but in Finland, by its most celebrated director, Aki Kaurismäki, with the title *Likaiset kädet*, in an icy staging, almost frozen as in this author's style, in which clashes and disagreements explode in a suffocating space and almost as a result of psychological self-blame.

This quick and purely indicative excursus on the relationship between Sartre and cinema is perhaps sufficient to indicate—as Chateau also points out in his essay—how misleading it is to attempt to identify in his screenplays or adaptations of his works the same existentialist or phenomenological substance that innervates his philosophical thought. In fact, Sartre himself was aware of the prevailing elusiveness of cinematic language and was fascinated by it precisely because, when confronted with a film, he ultimately perceived its narrative journey as something adventurous, as anything but "predetermined" for those who witness it, and who only at the end of the film can declare themselves as omniscient as the director, and thus rightfully "masters" of the film.

From this "obligatory finalization" of vision, as defined by the very nature of the medium, Sartre never derived certainty but only continuous and stimulating doubts and questions. Coming perhaps to the only conclusion that—in cinema as in life—"les jeux ne sont jamais faits."

Excerpts from Kierkegaard's Writings

And it is very sad, when considering the lives of men, that so many spend their entire lives in quiet perdition. They cease to live before the end of their lives, not in the sense that the content of their lives evolves later, and is then possessed in this evolution, but they end up living almost outside themselves, they disappear like shadows, their immortal soul is dissipated, and they are not frightened at the problem of its immortality, for they are already dissolved before they die. (*Either/Or*)

So I fight for freedom, for the future, for either/or. This is the treasure I intend to leave to those I love in the world. If my little son were now at the age of being able to understand me, and my last hour had come, I would say to him: I leave you neither substance nor titles nor honors; but I know where lies a treasure that can make you richer than anything in the world, and this treasure belongs to you, and for it you do not have to thank me, for I do not want your spirit to have to suffer in owing everything to one person: this treasure is buried within you, it is an either/or that makes men greater than angels. (*Either/Or*)

When all is silence around us, everything is as solemn as a night full of stars, when the soul stands alone in the midst of the world, in front of it appears not a remarkable man, but the eternal power itself, the sky almost opens wide, and the self chooses itself, or rather receives itself. In that instant the soul has seen the supreme height, that which no mortal eye can see and that which will never be forgotten, the personality receives the knight's banner, which ennobles it for eternity. Man does not become different from what he was before, he just becomes himself; consciousness coalesces, and he is himself. Just as an heir, even if he were heir to all the riches of this world, does not possess them before he comes of age, so the richest personality is nothing before he has chosen itself, and on the other hand, even what we might call the most miserable personality is everything when he has chosen itself. For greatness does not consist in being this or that, but in being oneself, and this anyone can do if he wants to. (*Either/Or*)

But what does it mean to live aesthetically, and what does it mean to live ethically? What is aesthetics in man, and what is ethics? To this I will answer: aesthetics in man is that by which he spontaneously is what he is; ethics is that by which he becomes what he becomes. (*Either/Or*)

He who lives aesthetically can give no satisfactory explanation of his life, because he lives always and only in the moment, and has only a relative and limited consciousness of himself. (*Either/Or*)

However, there still remains one stage, an aesthetic conception of life, the finest and most aristocratic of all. [...] This last conception of life is despair itself. It is a conception of aesthetic life, since the personality remains in its immediacy: it is *the last* conception of aesthetic life, since in a certain sense it has received within itself the consciousness of the nullity of itself. (*Either/Or*)

But what is this self? If I wanted to talk about a first moment, a first expression of it, my answer would be: it is the most abstract thing of all, which at the same time in itself is the most concrete—it is freedom. (*Either/Or*)

This "I," which he thus chooses is infinitely concrete, since it is himself; yet it is completely different from his previous "I," since he chose it absolutely. This "I" did not exist before, since it was created by choice; yet it existed since it was "himself." (*Either/Or*)

This is the profound reason why I was saying and continue to say that the either/or between aesthetic life and ethical life is not a perfect dilemma, because only one term can be chosen, and the other term arises from not choosing. With this choice, I choose not between good and evil, but I choose good, but while I choose good, I thereby choose the choice between good and evil. The original choice is always present in every subsequent choice. (*Either/Or*)

Despair then, and your lightness will no longer make you wander like an inconstant spirit, like a ghost in the ruins of a world that is also lost to you; despair, and your spirit will never again sigh in melancholy, for the world will again become beautiful and full of joys for you, though you will see it with different eyes than before, and your spirit, turned free, will rise up to the world of freedom. (*Either/Or*)

My thinking the absolute is the self-thinking of the absolute in me. (*Either/Or*)

One who lives ethically has, to recall an earlier expression, *memory* of his life; one who lives aesthetically does not have memory at all. He who lives ethically does not destroy the state of mind but considers it a moment; this moment saves him from living in the moment, this moment gives him mastery over pleasure. (*Either/Or*)

When the individual has grasped himself in his eternal value, it submerges him with all its fullness. The things of this world disappear for him. In the first instant an indescribable bliss fills him, giving him absolute confidence. (*Either/Or*)

Only when in choice one has possessed himself, has worn oneself, has penetrated oneself, totally, so that every movement is accompanied by the consciousness of responsibility, only then has one chosen oneself ethically, only then has one repented of oneself; only then is one concrete, only then is one's total isolation in absolute continuity with that reality to which one belongs. (*Either/Or*)

For when I, penitent, choose myself, I am concentrated in all my finite concreteness; and I remain in the most absolute continuity with it, when out of its finiteness I choose myself according to my infinitude. (*Either/Or*)

For he who lives aesthetically the old saying applies, "To be or not to be"; and the more aesthetically he is allowed to live, the more numerous are the conditions his life demands; and when he lacks only the smallest he is a dead man: he who lives ethically always has a way out; when everything is against him, when the darkness of the storm broods over him so that his neighbor no longer sees him, he therefore is not shipwrecked and there always remains a point to which he clings, this point is himself. (*Either/Or*)

Here I want to recall my definition of ethics: it is that by which man becomes what he becomes. It does not want the individual to become another, but himself; it does not want to destroy aesthetics, but to illuminate it. (*Either/Or*)

It is strange that with the word duty we end up thinking of an outward relationship, although the etymology of this word denotes an inward relationship: for what is imposed on me, not as a random individual, but according to my true being, lies, I believe, in the most intimate relationship with me. For duty is not an imposition, but something that is a task for the personality. When duty is seen in this way, the individual is rightly oriented in himself. (*Either/Or*)

Only when the individual himself is universal, does ethics allow itself to be translated into reality. (*Either/Or*)

He who has chosen and found himself ethically, has determined himself in all his concreteness. He then sees himself as an individual with certain gifts, certain passions, certain inclinations, certain habits, exposed to certain external influences, urged now in one direction, now in another. He sees himself as a task, and that task consists above all in ordering, educating, tempering, inflaming, repressing, in short, in achieving in the soul a balance, a harmony that is the fruit of personal virtues. (*Either/Or*)

Unconsciously, ethics is helpful to every man, but because it acts unconsciously, the aid of ethics takes on the appearance of a devaluation, as if it expresses only the pettiness of life, whereas it is an elevation, valuing the divinity of life. (*Either/Or*)

What constitutes the exceptional man, in a good sense, is the intensive force with which he is able to express what is human. What matters is to realize the universal with vivid intensity as soon as it is possible. If this succeeds, the man who is an exception will see his pain disappear again and dissolve into harmony. He understands that his position as an exception is only an expression of the limitedness of his individuality. He knows well that every man evolves with freedom, but he also knows that man does not create himself out of nothing and sees himself in his concreteness as his own task; he will reconcile himself with existence again when he understands that, in a sense, every man is an exception, and at the same time represents the human universal. (*Either/Or*)

I don't feel like anything. I don't feel like riding, it's too violent a motion; I don't feel like walking, it's too tiring; I don't feel like lying down, because either I would have to stay in that position, and I don't feel like it, or I would have to get up again, and I don't feel like it either. In conclusion: I don't feel like anything. (*Either/Or*)

Besides my other numerous acquaintances, I still have an intimate confidant: my melancholy. In the midst of my joy, in the midst of my work it beckons me, takes me in, though physically I remain inert. My melancholy is the most faithful lover I have known. And is it any wonder that I in turn love it? (*Either/Or*)

I say of my sorrow what the English say of their homes: my sorrow *is my castle*. Many regard being in pain as one of life's comforts. (*Either/Or*)

My soul is so grave that no thought can sustain it, no wing-stroke can lift it into the ether anymore. If it moves, it only passes skimming the earth, like birds flying low when a storm is coming. On my inner essence weighs a breathlessness, an anguish that foresees an earthquake. (*Either/Or*)

Thus I too am bound in a chain that is made up of dark fantasies, anguished dreams, restless thoughts, fearful forebodings, and unexplained anxieties. (*Either/Or*)

I lie there inert; the only thing I see is emptiness, the only thing I live by is emptiness, the only thing I move through is emptiness. Even less do I feel pain. Even pain has lost its consoling value for me. If I were offered all the wonders of the world or all the torments of the world, they would touch me in the same way; I would not turn away either to reach them or to flee them. I die death. And what could distract me? Yes, to be able to see a loyalty that would hold up to every trial, an enthusiasm that would endure everything, a faith that would move mountains; Conceive a thought that would connect the finite and the infinite. But the poisonous doubt of my soul corrodes everything. My soul is like the Dead Sea, over which no bird can fly, for having reached the middle of the way, it plummets exhausted into the mortal abyss. (*Either/Or*)

My soul has lost the possibility. If I were to wish something for myself, I would not wish wealth or strength, but the passion of possibility, that eye that eternally young, eternally ablaze, is worth the possibility everywhere. (*Either/Or*)

Every man naturally desires to act in this world according to his own strength, but from this follows in turn the desire to shape his forces in a specific direction, that in fact that best suits his individuality. But what is it? [...] It is not a simple crossroads, but a crossroads radiating in all directions. That's why it is so difficult to take the right one. It is perhaps precisely the misfortune of my existence, to be interested in too many things without getting to any decision: none of my interests is subordinate to the other, but they all hold hands. (*Journals*)

The highest thing you can do for a being, much higher than anything a man can do for it, is to set it free. (*Journals*)

In an earthly sense one may fall at the hands of another; in a spiritual sense one may fall only by his own hand—no one can ruin him but himself. (*Journals*)

Finite decisions are too small a thing for infinity to be able to get to them, so one must be forced into them. Being constrained is the only help of finitude. The choice of freedom, the only thing that saves in the realm of infinity! (*Journals*)

Could it be expressed with greater precision that freedom of choice is only a formal determination within freedom? And that the very accentuation of freedom of choice as such is the loss of freedom? The content of freedom is so decisive for freedom that the truth of freedom of choice is precisely to admit that there must be no choice here, although this is a choice. (*Journals*)

Certainly, necessity cannot produce freedom; but it can drive man's freedom to come as close as possible to the decisive act: wanting. (*Journals*)

Men fear truth more than death. (*Journals*)

Then, when they know the concrete reality of life better; when they have deepened awareness of their own finiteness; when age and the passage of time will have exerted all its power over them; when, despite all efforts, it will have become almost impossible to continue living with only the comfort of the thought of eternity; when—in a more humble sense—they will have become men, then they will glimpse the possibility of faith and believe through the strength of the absurdity that God will help them on this earth. (*Journals*)

What is believing? It is wanting in absolute reverent obedience, defending oneself against the vain thoughts of wanting to understand and against the vain delusions of being able to understand. (*Journals*)

"If you absolutely want reasons, I will gladly accommodate you. Do you want three, five, seven? You name it, how many do you want?" but I cannot say anything higher than this, "I believe." (*Journals*)

There is nothing else to do but to try to isolate, to pull the individual aside, to draw them existentially under the ideal. This is my task. (*Journals*)

Paradox is not a concession, but a "category": an ontological determination that expresses the relationship between an existing, knowing spirit and eternal truth. (*Journals*)

"Authority" does not consist in being king, emperor, general, possessing arms, being a bishop, police guard, etc., but in a firm and conscious resolution to sacrifice everything, even one's own life, for a cause, to want to defend this cause so as not to betray oneself, to need and fear nothing. This lack of regard for infinitude is "authority." True and proper authority is when this cause is truth. (*Journals*)

I am in the deepest sense an unhappy individuality. From the earliest years I have been nailed to a form of suffering bordering on insanity, which must have its deepest reason in the disproportion between my soul and my body. (*Journals*)

My misfortune, that is, what makes my life so arduous, is the fact that my tension is of a notch higher than that of other men; where I am, what I undertake has nothing to do with the single thing, but always with a principle and an idea. The majority thinks at most of a girl to marry: instead, I had to reflect on the essence of marriage. This applies to everything. (*Journals*)

Although I find myself immersed in reality to a degree like perhaps no one else here, in another sense I lived in a world of my own. [...] My suffering in a sense depends on the fact that I truly am not a man: I am too much spirit. (*Journals*)

And then when the sun has lowered its inquiring eye, when the story is over: not only will I wrap myself in my cloak, but I will cast over myself all night like a veil and I will come to join you—setting myself to listen, like a savage—not to spy your footsteps, but to feel the beats of your heart. (*Journals*)

If I became a writer I owe it essentially to it, to my melancholy and my money. Now, with God's help, I must become myself. (*Journals*)

Man hardly ever makes use of his true freedoms, for example freedom of thought; instead, freedom of speech is demanded in return! (*Journals*)

What drives one to begin is "wonder." What one begins with is "decision." (*Journals*)

But this wretched modern philosophy brought "reality" into logic and then, by distraction, one forgets that "reality" in logic is but "thought reality," that is, possibility. Art, science, poetry, etc. only have to do with possibility, that is, not in the sense of an idle hypothesis, but with possibility in the sense of ideal reality. (*Journals*)

Once doubt has penetrated, it lurks like cholera: any scientific defense only nurtures doubt. Only God and eternity are strong enough to master doubt (because doubt is precisely the force of man rebelling against God). But for God and eternity to master it, man must enter under the suction pump of the individual. (*Journals*)

All communication of truth has become an abstraction. The public has become an instance; The newspapers are called editing and the professors speculation; the pastor is meditation. No one has the courage to say, "I." But since the first condition of any communication of truth is indeed personality, since truth cannot take advantage of ventriloquism, one must resort to personality. In this situation to begin immediately with one's "I," while the world was so spoiled by never feeling an "I." was an impossible thing. My task has therefore been to create author personalities and throw them into the midst of reality of life to accustom men a little to speak in the first person. My action thus is that of a forerunner, until he who comes in the strictest sense says: I. Change course from this inhuman abstractness in order to be able to reach personality: Here is my task. (*Journals*)

"The individual." This principle can only be introduced poetically, because it would be shameless if one were to pose in an eminent sense as "the individual." It is therefore an aspiration. (*Journals*)

Existence always expresses what one believes. (*Journals*)

"The individual" is for man the determination of the spirit, of being a man: the crowd, the number, is the determination of animality. (*Journals*)

I am conscious of the fact that I exist, not that I have existed. (*Journals*)

Each individual is a world unto himself, possessing his own Holy of Holies, where no foreign hand can penetrate. (*Journals*)

Individuality must be explained as an infinite completion in an infinite becoming. (*Journals*)

What I miss is not being clear with myself about what I should do. It's part of my vocation, to understand, to see what God wants me to do; I need to find a truth that is the truth for me (for it's only then that man acquires an inner experience; but how many there are in whom the impression made by life resembles the figures that the sea draws on the sand, only to erase them a minute later), an idea for which I want to live and die. And what would it profit me to discover a supposedly objective truth, to study the systems of philosophers, and, when asked to expound on them, to find contradictions within each of them; what would it profit me to develop a theory of the state, and, from the details amassed here and there, to combine a whole, to build a world, a world in which I would not live, but which I would present to others as a spectacle; what would it profit me to be able to develop the meaning of Christianity, to explain many phenomena in detail, if this has no profound meaning for myself and my life? And the more I could do this, the more I would see others appropriating the fruits of my thought, the more desolate my situation would be, similar to that of parents whose poverty leads them to send their children away from them and entrust them to others. What use would it be to me if the truth stood before me, cold and naked, indifferent to whether I recognized it or not, arousing in me a shiver of anguish rather than confident abandonment? (*Journals*)

I don't want to deny that I still admit to an imperative of knowledge ... But then it must be welcomed in me in a living way; and this is what I now recognize as the main thing. This is what my soul thirsts for, like water in the Arabian deserts. This is what I lack. And that's why I remain like a man who has bought furniture, rented an apartment, but has not yet found the one who would share with him the joys and sorrows of life. To discover this idea, or rather to discover myself, there's no point in throwing myself further into the world ... That's what I was missing, to lead a complete human life and not just a life of knowledge, so that I could base the development of my thoughts, not on something called objective, something that is not a character of my own, but something that is united to the deepest root of my existence, through which I grow within the divine, something that is strongly united to it, even if the world were to fall apart. You see, this is what I'm lacking, and this is what I'm striving for. That's why I look with joy and inner comfort at the great men who have found this diamond, which they buy at the cost of their entire fortunes, even their lives. It's this inner action of man, this divine side of man, that we're talking about, not a heap of knowledge. (*Journals*)

What did I find? Not myself, but that's what I was looking for. (*Journals*)

It's no use for men to want to determine the exterior first, and only then the constituent element. One must first learn to know oneself before knowing anything else. (*Journals*)

Now I want to look at myself quietly, and act inwardly. For only in this way will I be able to say: me, to myself in a profound sense. (*Journals*)

Death and hell, I can forget everything, but not myself; I can't even forget myself in my sleep. (*Journals*)

Heaven is closed to those whose effort has limits. (*Journals*)

At that moment, I felt both my greatness and my smallness; these two great forces, pride and humility, had been amicably united. A marriage that was neither a marriage of reason, nor a misalliance, but in truth a silent union celebrated in the most secret chamber of the human heart, in the Holy of Holies. (*Journals*)

But there is an intuition of the world that paradox is higher than any system. (*Journals*)

Life is about having seen once, having felt once, something so incomparably great, that everything else seems like nothing: something you never forget, even if you forget everything else (Goethe). (*Journals*)

I have had extraordinary gifts; (ah! how I recognize myself in this preterit). Even when I feel most strongly about myself, I say: I have had … This is a unity of melancholy, reflection and fear of God; and this unity is my essence. (*Journals*)

I could pray for anything, except for the release of a deep suffering, which I've experienced since childhood, and which I understand belonged to my relationship with God. This suffering is exceptionality. (*Journals*)

I have my thorn in the flesh like Paul. That's why I couldn't enter general relationships; that's why I concluded that my task is extraordinary. (*Journals*)

Aristotle, Kant, precursors of the Kierkegaardian theory of being. Kant is thinking of existence that does not pass into the concept, of empirical existence. Existence corresponds to the individual who, following Aristotle's teaching, is outside the sphere of the concept. An individual man has no conceptual existence. (*Journals*)

If I am an authentic dialectician, if my essence is dialectical, I can only find rest in the ultimate term, not in any intermediary. (*Journals*)

But what use is science? Nothing. It destroys all tension, dissolving it in a quietly objective consideration, and so freedom becomes something inexplicable. ... One wonders whether he has it or not,—scientifically. He doesn't notice that he's lost it. (*Journals*)

Constraint cannot force the spiritual; at most, it can make it buy its freedom dearly. (*Journals*)

Anguish is the first reflex of possibility. (*Journals*)

Freedom can never be regained by reflection. It can only be regained through intensified fear and trembling: you can only save it and keep it by giving it back to God in full surrender and yourself in it. If you grieve deeply enough, you will have it back again. (*Journals*)

Isn't that a surprising and profound expression, that we can say: I have no choice, I choose this? What's more, Christianity can say to man: you can choose the only thing you need, in such a way that it's impossible to speak of choice. Thus, the fact that there is no choice is an expression of the immense passion or intensity with which one chooses. Could there be a clearer expression of the fact that freedom of choice is only a formal determination of freedom? (*Journals*)

Surprising as it may seem, it must be said that only fear, trembling and constraint can help man move towards freedom. For fear, trembling and constraint can master man in such a way that there can be no question of choice, and so one chooses what is right. In the moment of death, most men choose what must be chosen. ... Freedom exists only because, at the same moment, in the same second in which it is (freedom of choice), it hastens, with infinite haste, binding itself unconditionally by the choice of the gift of itself, the choice whose truth is: here, there can be no talk of choice. ... But man is not so completely spiritual. It seems to him that, since choice is left to him, he must take a little time ... Man lets himself be led astray by a ghost: freedom of choice. (*Journals*)

A Christian's existence is in contact with being. (*Journals*)

In our time, less importance is attributed to dreams … A simpler time believed that the unconscious life is the most powerful and profound of all. (*Journals*)

There are only two parties to choose between, and here lies the category of the One. (*Journals*)

Look at Socrates. […] He relates objectively to himself and speaks of himself as a third person. … He is subjectivity to the second power. He relates to objectivity as a true poet would relate to his poetic creation. This is a work of art. Otherwise, we are either an objective thing, or a mixture of contingency and arbitrariness; but to behave objectively in relation to our subjectivity, this is our task. The maximum that can be achieved from this point of view by a man can serve as an analogy—albeit a weak one—to give us a sense of God's infinite subjectivity. (*Journals*)

If man has to go into darkness, he naturally feels terror. What wonder is it that he is terrified before the unconditioned, of whom it can be said that no night, no darkness is half so dark, where all relative goals (mileposts, signs), where all goals (lanterns), where even the most delicate, intimate feelings of surrender, of self-giving are extinguished,—for otherwise the unconditioned is not the unconditioned? (*Journals*)

REFERENCES

AA. VV., *L'Esistenza nelle filosofie esistenziali*, a cura di A. Rizzacasa, Città Nuova, Roma 1976.

AA. VV., *Maschere kierkegaardiane*, a cura di L. Amoroso, Rosenberg and Sellier, Torino 1990.

AA. VV., *A Companion to Phenomenology and Existentialism*, edited by Hubert L. Dreyfus, and Mark A. Wrathall, Blackwell Pub: Malden, Massachusetts 2006.

AA. VV., *Studi Kierkegaardiani*, Morcelliana, Brescia 1957.

Abbagnano N., *Introduzione all'esistenzialismo*, Mondadori, Milano 1989.

Abbagnano N., *Possibilità e libertà*, Taylor, Torino 1956.

Adinolfi I., *Il cerchio spezzato*, Città Nuova, Roma 2000.

Amiel H.F., *Frammenti di un giornale intimo*, UTET, Torino 1967.

Bergson H., *Introduzione alla metafisica*, Laterza, Bari 1970.

Cantoni R., *La coscienza inquieta: Søren Kierkegaard*, Il Saggiatore, Milano 1976.

Carlisle C., *Philosopher of the heart, the restless life of Søren Kierkegaard*, Penguin Books, London 2020.

Chestov L., *Kierkegaard et la philosophie existentielle: (vox clamant in deserto)*, Librairie Philosophique J. Vrin, Paris 1948.

Chisholm R.M., *Realism and the Background of Phenomenology*, The Free Press, Glencoe, Illinois 1960.

Damiani R., *All'apparir del vero*, Mondadori, Milano 1998.

Detmer D., *Freedom as a Value. A Critique of the Ethical Theory of Jean-Paul Sartre*, Open Court Publishing Company, Illinois 1988.

Frankl V., *Logoterapia e analisi esistenziale*, Morcelliana, Brescia 1972.

© The Author(s), under exclusive license to Springer Nature
Switzerland AG 2023
R. Pugliese, *The Dizziness of Freedom in Kierkegaard and Sartre*,
https://doi.org/10.1007/978-3-031-38138-6

Fabro C., Jaspers et Kierkegaard, *Revue des Sciences Philosophiques et Théologiques* 1953, 37 (2), 209–52.

Ferreira M.J., *Kierkegaard*, John Wiley & Sons, Incorporated, Malden, Massachusetts, 2008.

Freud S., *Il disagio nella civiltà*, Einaudi, Torino 2010.

Galimberti U., *Heidegger, Jaspers e il tramonto dell'occidente*, Il Saggiatore, Milano 1996.

Gardiner P.L., *Kierkegaard*, Oxford University Press, Oxford 2002.

Guignon C., Pereboom D., *Existentialism – Basic writings*, Hackett Publishing Company, Indianapolis/Cambridge 2001.

Guicharnaud J., et al., *Sartre: A Collection of Critical Essays*, edited by E. Kern, Prentice-Hall, Englewood Cliffs, New Jersey 1962.

Hannay A., Marino G.D., *The Cambridge Companion to Kierkegaard*, Cambridge University Press, Cambridge 1997.

Hannay A., *Kierkegaard and Philosophy: Selected Essays*, Routledge, London 2003.

Heidegger M., *Metaphysical Foundations of Logic*, trans. Michael Heim, Indiana University Press, Bloomington, Indiana 1984.

Heidegger M., *Essere e tempo*, Longanesi, Milano 1976.

Husserl E., *La crisi delle scienze europee e la fenomenologia trascendentale*, Il Saggiatore, Milano 1997.

Jaspers K., *Filosofia dell'esistenza*, Bompiani, Milano 1943.

Jaspers K., *La questione della colpa. Sulla responsabilità politica della Germania*, Cortina Raffaello, Milano 1996.

Jaspers K., *Metafisica*, Mursia, Milano 1972.

Jolivet R., *Kierkegaard: alle fonti dell'esistenzialismo cristiano*, Edizioni Paoline, Roma 1960.

Judaken J., Bernasconi R., *Situating Existentialism: Key Texts in Context*, Columbia University Press, New York 2012.

Kaufmann K., *Existentialism: From Dostoevsky to Sartre*, New American Library, New York 1980.

Kierkegaard S., *Enten-Eller, V*, Adelphi, Milano 1989.

Kierkegaard S., *Aut-aut*, Mondadori, Milano 2015.

Kierkegaard S., *Il concetto dell'angoscia – La malattia mortale*, Sansoni, Firenze 1973.

Kierkegaard S., *Diario*, Rizzoli, Milano 2019.

Kierkegaard S., *Stadi sul cammino della vita*, Rizzoli, Milano 2001.

Lowrie W., "Existence" as Understood by Kierkegaard and/or Sartre, *The Sewanee Review* 1950, 58 (3), 379–401.

Lukács G., *La distruzione della ragione*, Einaudi, Torino 1959.

Macquarrie J., *In Search of Humanity: A Theological and Philosophical Approach*, S.C.M, London 1984.

Mcbride W.L., *Existentialist Background: Kierkegaard, Dostoevsky, Nietzsche, Jaspers*, Heidegger, Garland, New York 1997.

Marcel G., Hanley K.R., *Gabriel Marcel's Perspectives on the Broken World*, Marquette University Press, Milwaukee, Wisconsin 1998.

Marcel G., *L'uomo problematico*, Borla, Roma 1992.

May R., *The Meaning of Anxiety*, Hauraki Publishing, San Francisco, California 2015.

May R., *Psicologia esistenziale*, Astrolabio, Roma 1970.

Mead M., *L'adolescenza in Samoa*, Giunti, Firenze 2017.

Melchiorre V., *Saggi su Kierkegaard*, Marietti, Genova 1987.

Mészáros I., *The work of Sartre: search for freedom and the challenge of history*, Monthly Review Press, New York 2012.

Michelman S., *The A to Z of Existentialism*, Scarecrow Press, Lanham, Maryland 2010.

Mooney E.F., *Ethics, Love, and Faith in Kierkegaard: Philosophical Engagements*, Indiana University Press, Bloomington, Indiana 2008.

Mura G., *Angoscia ed esistenza*, Città Nuova, Roma 1981.

Pareyson L., *Kierkegaard e Pascal*, Mursia, Milano 1998.

Pareyson L., *Studi sull'esistenzialismo*, Sansoni, Firenze 1971.

Pascal B., *Pensieri*, Bompiani, Milano 2000.

Reale G., *Valori dimenticati dell'Occidente*, Bompiani, Milano 2004.

Riva F., *Essere e avere di Marcel e il dibattito su esistenza ed essere nell'esistenzialismo*, Paravia, Torino 1990.

Reynolds J., *Understanding Existentialism*, Routledge, London 2014.

Santoni R.E., *Bad Faith, Good Faith and Authenticity in Sartre's Early Philosophy*, Temple University Press, Philadelphia, Pennsylvania 1985.

Sartre J.-P., *La trascendenza dell'ego*, Marinotti Edizioni, Milano 2012.

Sartre J.-P., *L'esistenzialismo è un umanismo*, Mursia, Milano 1946.

Sartre J.-P., *L'essere e il nulla*, Il Saggiatore, Milano 2014a.

Sartre J.-P., *The Philosophy of Existentialism: Selected Essays*, Philosophical Library/Open Road, New York 2014b.

Schrader G.A., *Existential Philosophers: Kierkegaard to Merleau-Ponty*, McGraw-Hill, New York 1967.

Schrag C.O., *Existence and Freedom: Towards an Ontology of Human Finitude*, Northwestern University Press, Evanston, Illinois 1961.

Simont J., La lutte du maître et de l'esclave dans Cahiers pour une morale et Critique de la raison dialectique, in *"Etudes Sartriennes"*, 4, 1990.

Stewart J., *Kierkegaard and Existentialism*, Routledge, London 2011.

Velocci G., *Filosofia e fede in Kierkegaard*, Città Nuova, Roma 1976.

Wahl J., *Études Kierkegaardiennes*, Librairie Philosophique J. Vrin, Paris 1967.

Wahl J., *Kierkegaard – L'Un devant l'Autre*, Hachette, Paris 1998.

Wahl J., *Breve storia dell'esistenzialismo*, Mimesis, Milano 2017.

Wahl J., *Existence humaine et transcendance*, Neuchatel, La Baconnière 1944.

Wahl J., *Les Philosophies de l'existence*, Armand Colin, Paris 1959.

Webber J., *The Existentialism of Jean-Paul Sartre*, Routledge, New York 2009.

Weston M., *Kierkegaard and Modern Continental Philosophy: An Introduction*, Routledge, London 1994.

Wilcocks R., *Critical Essays on Jean-Paul Sartre*. G.K. Hall, Boston 1988.

Wood P.R., *Understanding Jean-Paul Sartre*, University of South Carolina Press, South Carolina 1990.

Zaner R.M., Ihde D., *Phenomenology and Existentialism*, Putnam, New York 1973.

INDEX[1]

A
Amiel, Henri-Frédéric, 42, 44
Aristotle, 4, 5, 38, 54, 80, 81

B
Bergson, Henri, 35
Breton, André, 26

C
Cantoni, Remo, 13, 14
Comte, Auguste, 20, 20n4
Copernicus, 43

D
Dostoevsky, Fëdor, 20, 55

E
Einstein, Albert, 26
Epictetus, 5

F
Foucault, Michel, 48, 52
Freud, Sigmund, ix, 26
Frost, Robert, 22, 23

H
Hegel, Georg Wilhelm
    Friedrich, v, 1, 22,
    32–35
Heidegger, Martin, 6, 26, 33, 34,
    37–39, 45, 49–52, 56
Husserl, Edmund, 45, 46

J
Jaspers, Karl, 31, 33, 58n12, 59
Jung, Carl, 39

K
Kafka, Franz, 26
Kant, Immanuel, 2, 7, 43–46, 80

[1] Note: Page numbers followed by 'n' refer to notes.

Printed in the United States
by Baker & Taylor Publisher Services